# PRAISE FOR *THE CHOCOLATE-COVERED UMBRELLA*

Tilda Norberg has given us an inspiring and exciting book about working with dreams. *The Chocolate-Covered Umbrella* not only contains remarkably skillful teaching of powerful methods for making dreams relevant in a psychological setting, but it also carries Fritz Perls's revolutionary Gestalt dreamwork much further into the realm of personal spiritual revelation. Tilda's delightful style of dreamworking and her lightly humorous touch in reporting her own dreams mark her book as a major advancement in the psychology of dreams.

—ROBERT K. HALL, MD
Psychiatrist, published poet, lay Buddhist priest
Cofounder of The Lomi School and Lomi Clinic
Santa Rosa, California

Tilda Norberg's process is transformative. I should know; I learned it at some of her workshops and have used it for years. It connected me to the sacred presence within, enabling me to become the person I dreamed of being. For anyone looking to tap into his or her inherent creativity, *The Chocolate-Covered Umbrella* is a "must" read. I loved this book!

—ANNE MIMI SAMMIS
Artist and host of *Mimi's Art Studio* on PBS

Edifying, serendipitous, and enlivening, *The Chocolate-Covered Umbrella* rang with truth and power for me, producing a vista of self-awareness and healing with personal and spiritual growth.

—STEVEN L. GAROFOLO, PhD
Teacher

Once alienated from the church, I clung to the simplicity of dream analysis and remained only in the shallows of actual dreamwork. After learning that I can pray my dreams, I am discovering transforming truth time after time that makes my life richer than I thought possible. Through *The Chocolate-Covered Umbrella*, Tilda Norberg's teaching has set me free to discover the depths of the Holy within and beyond.

—KRISTIN AARDEMA FAIGH
Spiritual Growth and Healing Minister
Lake Harbor United Methodist Church
Muskegon, Michigan

# The Chocolate-Covered Umbrella

## Discovering Your Dreamcode

Tilda Norberg

FRESH AIR BOOKS™
Nashville

Cover illustration: Aaron Grayum
Cover design: Left Coast Design, Portland, Oregon
Interior design: Aaron Grayum / Tinymusicbox Design
First printing: 2009

**Library of Congress Cataloging-in-Publication Data**
Norberg, Tilda.
  The chocolate-covered umbrella : discovering your dreamcode / Tilda Norberg.
     p.  cm.
  ISBN 978-1-935205-02-9
  1. Dreams—Religious aspects—Christianity. 2. Dream interpretation. 3. Gestalt psychology. I. Title.
  BR115.D74N67 2008
  248.2'9—dc22

                                                          2008029241

Printed in the United States of America

# CONTENTS

# INTRODUCTION

Each time you sleep, you could receive the gift of a dream that will change your life. Your dreams send you nightly invitations to grow, invitations so precisely tailored to fit you that they are delivered in a code only you can break. Dreams spring from your feelings and fears, your scars and strengths, your hidden depths and desires—every nuance of your life that makes you unique. Furthermore, your dreams provide a venue for the Holy One to act. Dreams are God speaking your language.

Dreams can challenge you to

- discover or integrate parts of yourself
- change your priorities
- face your dragons
- embrace greater depth of love and compassion
- surrender to the Love that surrounds you and is still creating you

You may sense that your dreams are important, but when you first wake from a dream full of puzzling images, weird plots, or heart-thumping danger, you probably just feel relieved to be back in real life. "Whew! What a crazy dream," you tell yourself as you crawl from under the covers. You are uneasy when life seems out of control, even in your dreams. You like feeling that your world is somewhat predictable. No wonder some people dismiss their dreams as fluff and moonbeams, while others fear that their dreams prove that they are finally losing it.

Although welcoming your dreams isn't always easy, before you dismiss them, why not find out whether they have something important to say? For a time, let yourself be intrigued with discovering their messages. Be open to the wisdom of your dreamcode. If you are spiritually hungry, you might decide to keep alert for God's activity in your dreams. See for yourself if your dreams are worth some time and effort.

> **Instead of interpreting your dreams, you will learn to play with them.**

If you are new to dreamwork, this probably feels like a big, vague-sounding challenge. I imagine you thinking, *Yeah, right! Just how do I make sense of my screwy dreams, much less find God in there?* In our culture, many thoughtful people believe that genuine understanding of dreams is complicated and can be revealed only by psychoanalysis. My opinion: just as you don't need a doctor to tell you that good nutrition and exercise will maximize your physical health, you don't need a degree in psychology to connect meaningfully with your dreams. Nor do you necessarily need to be in psychotherapy.

In *The Chocolate-Covered Umbrella* I will show you a simple and holistic way to encounter your dreams and use them to grow emotionally and spiritually. For years I have led workshops on dreamwork for ordinary people, and many have made personal discoveries almost right away. If you decide to take this ride, you will need a spirit of adventure, curiosity, and willingness to do a bit of inner sleuthing. As you follow the suggestions in *The Chocolate-Covered Umbrella*, you will also need to stop trying to figure out your dreams, attacking them with reason and logic. Instead of interpreting your dreams, you will learn to play with them. In other words, you will learn how to open yourself to the rich discoveries that can come from playful interaction with your dream images, all the while paying attention to your body, your hunches, and your experience of the here and now. I will offer step-by-step suggestions to show you how.

I expect that your dreamwork will not only begin to nurture your emotional growth but will also lead you to spiritual awakening. You may be invited not only to wake up and smell the coffee but also to wake up to the Love that will not let you go.

Gestalt Pastoral Care, or GPC, is my synthesis of Gestalt work with Christian spirituality and healing prayer. Dreamwork is a small but crucial part of GPC's holistic approach, and it's one of my personal favorites when I myself feel stuck.

To tell you that I work full-time with GPC as a United Methodist minister doesn't convey the wonderful delight I feel as I watch people grow and heal. Daily I am moved by the spiritual hunger, the bravery, the honesty, the desire to live fully, the profound beauty of those on a conscious spiritual and emotional quest. Much of my "work" seems like midwifery—I simply wait to see what will happen next and then suggest ways for the one "in labor" to cooperate with a process that is already in motion. (Often the only thing I need to say is, "Breathe!") Always I am awed by the Holy One who, astonishingly, seems to be orchestrating the whole affair.

Psychiatrist Fritz Perls (1893–1970), who called himself the "finder" of Gestalt therapy, would be horrified at the way I combine Gestalt and spirituality. A cantankerous genius, Perls didn't allow religion into his world. I believe, however, that his work is an electrical socket, and the plug that just fits is Christian spirituality that includes a focus on healing. When a connection is made, the light goes on.

In spite of Perls's antagonism toward religion, he edged toward spirituality despite himself. He found that if people were willing to cultivate acute awareness of the here and now—rather than just talk about their lives—they made rapid progress. He began to trust more deeply each person's innate drive to grow. As he grew older, he became more holistic. Increasingly his work became more powerful and simpler as he discovered that psychoanalysis was not the only show in town. Many people fortunate enough to work with Fritz often reported that just one session with him triggered a lasting transformation.

I began learning about Gestalt in 1966 just after graduating from Union Theological Seminary in New York City. Back then I was in big emotional and spiritual trouble. I had become increasingly depressed and angry when I discovered that even though ordination of women had been official policy for ten years, the Methodist Church did not, in actual practice, welcome women clergy. I wondered if I had just wasted three years on a difficult graduate degree, or if I had some big flaw that made me unfit for ministry. For a while Gestalt was my personal lifeline as I dealt with my confusion over what I believed was a true calling, my anger at God and especially at the church, and my irrational guilt that beat me up with the accusation that joblessness was entirely my fault.

Gestalt dreamwork played an important role in my healing process. As I became more whole, I began to see just how beautifully Gestalt fits with good spiritual direction, the ministry of healing, and pastoral care—despite Perls's opinions about religion. Praying my own dreams, I came to believe that prayerful dreamwork could be a gift not only to church folk but also to those outside the church who hunger for a new way to open to God.

I must make clear that while GPC dreamwork is not psychotherapy, you may encounter some feelings that surprise or scare you. Actually, it's okay to be a bit anxious sometimes. Growth often involves fear, because change itself can be scary. Remember that you can take the dreamwork process slowly or stop altogether. Also remember that your dreams usually don't flood you with material you are not strong enough to face. Keep in mind, though, that you may discover you need some outside help. Don't hesitate to see a professional—a psychotherapist, pastoral counselor, or spiritual director—just as you would see a doctor if your nasty cold seems to be veering off toward pneumonia. Asking for appropriate help is just another way your dreams can prompt you to become more whole.

> **"Dreamwork is a lot like making art; the process can take time and be a bit messy. "**

When doing dreamwork by yourself, you may find it handy to know how to shut the door deliberately on an emotion or memory you don't want to experience right now. Don't worry; your feelings won't vanish just because you shut them down for a while. You can always come back to them later. Shutting down *with awareness* can actually be a wonderfully positive step in your growth; you can learn as much from a clear no as you can from a yes. In the appendix I suggest some ways to shut down your emotions temporarily.

Most of the dream stories in *The Chocolate-Covered Umbrella* are actual dreams I've shared with the permission of the dreamers, whose identities have been disguised. A few of the dreams that appear in this book were first published in *Consenting to Grace: An Introduction to Gestalt Pastoral Care*, a book I finished in 2006. Several dream stories are composites, that is, I have combined some similar dreams into one narrative. Occasionally I have imagined a dream to illustrate a point.

Dreamwork is a lot like making art; the process can take time and be a bit messy. You play around with approaches; you wait for an "aha!" You pray for inspiration. You start again. You stop to rest and mull things over. You muddle your way along; you toss out some directions and develop others. Eventually you find your way, and things fall into place. New patterns emerge, relationships change, knots are untangled, more "ahas" come. You can never anticipate exactly how it will turn out, so expect surprises.

# INTRODUCING GPC DREAMWORK

## THE CHOCOLATE-COVERED UMBRELLA

With a bemused and slightly embarrassed grin, Marvin, a well-respected university professor and advocate for social reform, read the following dream from his journal:

> I am at a big gathering for social activists from all over the world. We are having an awards ceremony when suddenly I am called to the podium. I am not expecting an award, but I make my way to the front of the banquet hall. There I am formally thanked for the support I have given over the years to movements for world peace, fair-trade practices, labor unions, racial and gender equality, and economic justice.
>
> I am then presented with my surprise award: a beautiful, amazing, full-size chocolate-covered umbrella. Somehow I know that my new umbrella is from Czechoslovakia. Everyone claps and carries on while I just stand there staring at the weirdest, silliest award ever. I've never had a chocolate-covered Czechoslovakian umbrella before, that's for sure, but I like my new umbrella a lot. I wake up feeling delighted and curious.

As I listened to Marvin's dream, I felt my own delight at the fascinating creativity of image and story that rises spontaneously during sleep. Marvin, with his brilliant mind and scholarly bent, probably wouldn't have thought up a chocolate-covered Czechoslovakian umbrella, but there it was, freshly sprung from his brain the night before, captivating us with its secrets, invitations, and sheer offbeat wackiness. The dream itself drew our first response. Marvin and I entered his dream world with appreciation, curiosity, and a lot of laughter. Our natural, unstudied response to the dream paved the way for the next steps in his dreamwork.

I didn't ask what Marvin thought an umbrella might symbolize or what umbrellas or chocolate meant to him. I didn't ask how he felt about Czechoslovakia or if he had ever been there. I didn't inquire if he had attended a big meeting recently. I didn't scan the files in my own mind about the function of umbrellas or the role of chocolate in human experience. *In fact, neither of us speculated about the possible meaning of the dream.* Instead, I asked Marvin to enter even more fully into the dream reality and playfully describe himself as the chocolate-covered umbrella, pretending for a few moments that the umbrella itself could talk. Marvin readily agreed, and almost immediately he was surprised to find that he was exploring a newly emerging part of himself.

"I taste good," Marvin said as the umbrella.

Everyone likes me; what's not to like about chocolate? My goodness, I'm delicious! I'm playful and crazy and amazing. I am a very unusual gift wrapped in a colorful package. I'm sure I'm the only one like me in the world. And who knew? I have Czechoslovakian roots.

After a pause, the umbrella spoke to Marvin.

I come from an exotic place, somewhere you've never been, but Marvin, you really do need to go there. I have a very complicated mechanism that can help you fly. I'm the kind of umbrella that lifts you up above the rooftops, sort of like the umbrella in *Mary Poppins*. I see magnificent views from way up high. It's almost transcendent up there. I think what I see must be something like the view that God has. When I say that, I sound kinda theological.

I really like being a chocolate-covered umbrella. I can do my part to shelter people and maybe bring others along with me so they can have this view too and see a little like God.

Marvin paused again, startled and moved by what he heard himself saying. He remained silent for a few minutes, eyes closed, breathing deeply, feeling his "umbrella-ness." After a few minutes I asked him if he would switch roles and react to the umbrella's words.

Marvin spoke as himself:

I'm really intrigued with you, Chocolate Umbrella. I love chocolate, but I always thought chocolate wasn't good for me. For you to show up in my dream is pretty interesting. What's going on here?

He paused and then added with a grin:

Hey, professors are supposed to be serious, or at least dignified. I wouldn't get much done if I just flew around all day like Mary Poppins. . . . The social structures that grind people up bring on tremendous suffering. They are not trivial or funny, so why would anyone give you to me? You seem like a sort of weird, whimsical joke, Umbrella. I have to admit, though, it would be great fun to fly!

The umbrella answered,

So learn to fly! Have fun! And stop looking a gift horse in the mouth!

Marvin:

But I do have fun. I really enjoy my days off. I love being with my wife and children and grandchildren. I like to travel and go out to dinner. I like to attend concerts and plays, and I do all these things.

Umbrella:

There is more, much more. You don't know it yet, but you need me. Here's an idea: Try bringing me to work with you.

Again Marvin paused as he allowed thoughts and feelings to wash over him. "Bring a chocolate umbrella to work . . . " I waited. Then he said, "I'm wondering about the man who called me to the podium, the award presenter. I think he is important, but I don't know why. Who is he, and why would he be in charge of such a crazy scene?" I suggested that Marvin play the role of presenter and simply pay attention to what happened.

Marvin spoke as the presenter:

> Marvin, I have chosen something very special, something just right for you. A chocolate-covered umbrella may seem strange at first, but trust me, it will open some new worlds for you. It takes faith to let a chocolate-covered umbrella take you flying, and I want you to have faith. So have fun; be colorful; see your new umbrella as a gift and not a burden. . . . I want to lift your burdens instead of giving you another one. I want you to know that you don't have to do everything yourself. I will be there to help you.

He trailed off into silence, letting old patterns of thought and behavior rearrange themselves. At last he said,

> As I learn to fly, maybe I can learn to hold my intellectual constructs more loosely. Maybe, just maybe, I don't have to worry so much about always being perfectly prepared for everything. Really, I always overprepare, even after all these years! My dream is telling me that it's time to give up asking myself, "Have I done enough? Is everything neatly arranged? Have I planned everything down to the last detail?" . . .
>
> I believe God is inviting me to give up my earthbound, tough-it-out perfectionism. And inviting me to remember that I have been given a special gift.

Louder now and laughing, Marvin verbally underlined each word:

> After all, I am a one-of-a-kind! chocolate-covered! flying! Czechoslovakian! holy! umbrella!—whoo-ee!

In the following weeks Marvin often deliberately recalled his extraordinary dream. As best he could, he "took his new umbrella to work" and began to notice small but important changes. He was more spontaneous in his teaching, more relaxed with preparation, more trusting of his experience and skills, and more intentional about taking breathing spaces even during periods of intense focus and pressure. He reminded himself many times a day that he was just now learning to fly, and to go easy on himself. As he put it, he began to move from "squeezing to flying."

## WINGING IT

A second dream soon confirmed Marvin's growth. In this new dream, he visits a beautiful old Lutheran church in Germany. A service is about to begin, but the pastor has not shown up. Minutes before the service is to begin, Marvin is asked to step in. This invitation is a big challenge; he is not a Lutheran, has never led worship before, and must speak in his rusty German. He agrees anyway. "It is all very hasty and thrown together," says Marvin. "I don't even know what the readings are, and I'm shuffling around in my mind how to begin when I remember that in German Lutheran churches the pastor says, *"Im Namen des Vaters, und des Sohnes, und des Heiligen Geistes.* Amen." (In the name of the Father and of the Son and of the Holy Spirit.) I start with that, and off I go."

> All through the service I am not sure what I am doing, but it doesn't seem to matter. I'm surprised that I'm so confident. I'm not perfect; I make a lot of mistakes, but I laugh at them. I'm doing what I can, and I'm okay. The congregation is singing with heart and responding well to the service.
> The most remarkable thing of all is that while I am still asleep, I sense that I am a chocolate umbrella. I am aware that right now I am flying in the middle of ecclesiastical chaos. I'm literally winging it. What a wonderful experience! When I wake up, I have a feeling of great freedom and joy.

The "flying lessons" in Marvin's dreams beautifully illustrate the principles of GPC (Gestalt Pastoral Care) Dreamwork. Later on I will explain in much more detail the theory behind the approach and how to use it to work with your own dreams. For now, here are some things to notice:

First, Marvin and I let ourselves react naturally to the nuttiness of the umbrella dream. We took it lightly and encountered it playfully. We laughed at his Lutheran ecclesiastical chaos. Although we did not pray during Marvin's work with either dream, we could easily have done so, giving thanks for the zany images and the growth that dreams can bring.

> ❝ Dreams don't emerge from our rational minds; immediately attempting to stuff dreams into rational categories and associations is cumbersome and sometimes even futile. ❞

Second, as I have already pointed out, Marvin and I didn't discuss the possible meaning of his dreams or try to make associations with his life. We didn't engage with the question Marvin raised about why the presenter was important. In other words, we didn't try to interpret or analyze his dream. Why not? The short answer is that dreams don't emerge from our rational minds; immediately attempting to stuff dreams into rational categories and associations is cumbersome and sometimes even futile. More about this later, I promise.

Third, by interacting playfully with the symbols in his dream, Marvin was open to *making discoveries* instead of *making sense*. He became the umbrella, the presenter, and himself in the dream and allowed each of them to have a voice and talk to each other. Just telling his "Winging It" dream as if it were actually happening in the present helped him experience his dream, rather than merely talk about it.

Fourth, the assumption behind playing the different parts in a dream is that nearly every person, object, and idea in Marvin's dream is uniquely shaped by parts of Marvin's being. Almost certainly Marvin would have made even more discoveries if he had also played the roles of the audience, the banquet hall, and Czechoslovakia. If Marvin works with the dream again and plays the chocolate-covered umbrella for the second or third time, undoubtedly his discoveries will deepen and acquire more nuances. Someday he might also play the missing pastor in "Winging It," or the congregation, or the magnificent old Gothic church, or Germany itself. (Marvin seems to specialize in dreaming about countries.) We can expect that all these symbols will be rich with personal meaning for Marvin.

Fifth, because Marvin's personal dreamcode is just that, *personal*, Marvin is the one who can best discover the message of his dream.

Sixth, we were attentive to the possibility that God was involved in Marvin's growth and might well be present somehow in his dream. Marvin was profoundly challenged by the Presenter, who invited him to have faith, lighten up, and quit trying to be so perfect. The Presenter didn't identify himself as God, but surely he carried a whiff of God's presence in his gracious message.

Seventh, the two dreams together presented icons that illumined a larger process of lifelong growth.

Finally, my role with Marvin was simple. Other than suggesting that he play various parts in his dreams, I was there mostly as witness and listener. I gave him space and silence when he stopped talking. Occasionally I asked him to repeat a sentence or two if something he said struck me as important. I prayed silently as he went along. What I *didn't* do was analyze, ask questions, interpret, or supply answers.

# YOU *Are* HARDWIRED *for* LIFELONG GROWTH

## THE FORGOTTEN ATTIC

My almost-three-year-old grandson lives with such intensity and vigor that he takes my breath away. Whatever Silas does involves his full attention and energy, whether it is racing up the stairs, daring to go down the slide alone, learning to write his name, pasting stickers in his sticker book, pretending to be a doggie, memorizing the names and personality traits of every friend of Thomas the Tank Engine, or typing words into the computer. Shivering with delight all the way, Silas is playing full-time to master his own body and the world he inhabits with the dedication of an artist or a monk.

Like Silas, you were born with a drive to grow, and this drive always stays with you, through every age and life stage, every hard knock, every twist of your life story, during the good times as well as the bad. You may not always *feel* the urgency to grow, but be assured that your deepest self is biologically predisposed toward healing and wholeness of body, mind, emotions, and spirit. Underneath your fear and inertia you are a valiant wildflower that insists on blooming, even when you find yourself rooted in a cracked cement driveway.

It may be easier to imagine your own drive toward health if you think of what happens when you slice your finger in the kitchen. You wash your cut, spray an antibiotic on it, but even before the Band-Aid is in place, your body has already surged into rescue mode. Dozens of different kinds of cells, hormones, coagulation factors, and other chemicals trigger a series of rapid, interrelated changes, each one setting off the next and the next and the next, creating an exquisitely intricate process called the immune cascade. Imagine that, a *cascade* of help, just for a small cut! A serious injury or illness activates a veritable tidal wave of immensely complex processes, focused first on helping you survive, and then on getting you well. Even though physical healing does not always occur, your truly amazing body does a magnificent job of fighting for health.

> " Underneath your fear and inertia
> you are a valiant wildflower
> that insists on blooming. "

Now here is the leap I'm asking you to make: *A similar healing process makes emotional and spiritual growth possible.* If you experience the death of a loved one, for example, your whole self mobilizes to get you through your grief. Hot tears come unbidden. Painful memories flood in. You may be awash with guilt and regrets. You are exhausted, but your mind races when you lie down. You feel needy, helpless, unable to make decisions. Almost anything can trigger waves of sadness that crash in on you. Memories bear down on you, and you find yourself telling the same stories again and again. You may find that prayer is a lifeline, or you may be mad as a rattlesnake at God.

Your constant turmoil almost compels you to stay involved in the chaotic upheaval inside you. You may need support, a listening companion who believes that your natural process is taking you toward healing. If you are willing to go through, instead of avoiding, your own experience, you will probably realize one day that you are feeling less raw and devastated. Somehow you have made room for profound loss. The terrible movies in your head don't plague you as often. The sun feels warm again, and you find yourself taking pleasure in walks, gentle times with good friends, or working in the garden. You grow to forgive yourself for words you said to your loved one, and for those you didn't. You may ask God for forgiveness, and you may even be ready to give up your anger toward God. You may find that your faith has been strengthened, or even birthed, by the fire you've gone through. Painful memories are slowly transformed into treasured memorials to the staying power of love. In time you will be able to go on with your life, even find happiness again. Your natural inner process has led you toward emotional and spiritual healing.

Now here's the catch: it is easy, and often much more comfortable in the short run, to ignore or deny your emotions and spirit. You can act as though nothing is wrong; you can stifle your impulses to cry or laugh or remember or pray. You can pretend that there are no ripples in your pond, and maybe not even any depths. You can pull up your socks and just go on doing what you always do. After a time you don't feel much at all.

Alternatively, you can become so attached to feeling awful that after a while you wear an invisible sweatshirt that proclaims, "I am in pain!" Your tragedy defines you and helps you hold on to the familiar past. Keeping yourself in pain is a way to stay connected to all you have lost. Instead of walking through the storm, you hunker down inside it, resisting any possibility of feeling better. This, too, affords protection of a sort. You feel bad, but at least you don't have to weather yet another big change.

Shutting down or hunkering down *temporarily* is not a bad thing but actually a wonderful gift. Occasionally shielding yourself from your inner uproar during times of crisis can keep you sane and allow you to deal with one thing at a time. It keeps you from being flooded with emotions that feel too big to contain in your body. Pat yourself on the back for learning how to shut down! You found a way to shield yourself from inner chaos that you sense could overwhelm you.

But here is the problem. When "temporary" merges into many months or even years, you stop growing. Now shutting down has become automatic, pervasive, a way of life. What was once a great help to your emotional stability now separates you from yourself and from possibilities for healing and growth. No longer do you easily connect with your inborn urgency to keep maturing. You miss out on a lot of zesty living, even joy. Growth is not always about getting through terrible pain. Most often it involves change, perhaps only a small shift in awareness or embracing a good part of you that got lost. Learning to love yourself and others more deeply, opening to the tender joy of pregnancy and birth, meeting the challenge of a new job, or being creative in retirement is most certainly growth too. So is surrendering a grudge, making room for forgiveness to take root, or learning to pray from your heart.

If you have habitually shielded yourself from change, even the most wonderful possibility, such as falling in love with a special person, can leave you feeling afraid, self-conscious, or stuck. Though you long to feel more alive, you discover that you have quashed not only your pain and fear but also your healthy anger, exuberance, spontaneity, artistry, daring, trust, and capacity for delight.

Children grow in a hundred ways, but all too often grown-ups simply age. What makes the habits of living a muted existence so tenacious? I believe there are several interrelated explanations:

*First, you may have had some experiences that have made you reluctant to be your real self.* You may have been criticized, teased, ignored, berated, or taught to believe that the world is a terribly dangerous place. Your feelings may have been discounted. You may have felt unloved and unprotected. Perhaps you were abused, your innocence stolen. Maybe you suffered other big losses. Perhaps you made a bad mistake and you're afraid to try again. Rapid changes may have jostled you so much that you crave predictability and sameness. For many different reasons, you have learned how to insulate yourself because of fear that ancient feelings could overwhelm you. You know how to not feel, not remember, not care—at least some of the time.

> "Your dreams are both powerful and rebellious. . . . They are free to take you to interior places you can't imagine and challenge the way you run your life —and the way your life runs you."

*Second, you may be afraid of your healthy self.* What might happen if all that intensity and vigor inside you got loose? Would you destroy something or make a big and very public mistake? If you recognize your strength, energy, and special gifts, you might have to risk doing something you've always dreamed about. If you allow yourself to fly your own version of a chocolate umbrella, who would soar around up there with you? Will those still on the ground be jealous or threatened or stop loving you? Will everyone point up at you and say, "Look at that, will ya? Weird, huh?"

*Third, you may fear growth and change itself.* You may believe that if you change, you will lose your very identity. The wispy question that doesn't quite come to awareness is, "Who would I be if I weren't in pain, anxious, flighty, victimized, weak, angry, nice, helpful, in control, or _____?" (You fill in the blank.) Let's be frank: human growth can be a scary and unpredictable journey, and growing takes effort, energy, and attention. You may feel so tired and battered that you are just happy to get through the day without having to cope with changes. Truly, the deadness or suffering you already know can seem better, and certainly safer, than the healing you can't yet imagine.

*Finally, your very competence and relative wholeness can hinder your continued growth.* Perhaps you have found a way to make your life work. You are reasonably happy and are pretty good at your job. You pay your bills, take care of your car, raise your kids, roll along with your marriage, appear at social occasions. Your house is clean enough that no one is coming down with dysentery, and your laundry gets done before you have to buy new underwear. Unless you are challenged by a crisis, it is ever so easy to pedal a stationary bicycle for years.

With all these good reasons to put your growth process on hold, it may be hard to jump-start your natural healing process. Even though you sense there is more for your life, you may not know how to get moving.

Here is where your dreams can be a tremendous help. Your dreams are both powerful and rebellious. They are not bound by your fears, inertia, pain, or what your grandmother said about you. They don't have to fit your cramped idea of who you think you are. They don't have to be reasonable, nor do they have to please your parents, your boss, or the church. They are free to take you to interior places you can't imagine and challenge the way you run your life—and the way your life runs you. They can be outrageous, daring, playful, zany, sexy. They speak truth as they point to your particular needs for growth. They highlight the changes you are now strong enough to make. Your dreams are full of parts of you that you have denied, disguised in your own easily decipherable dreamcode. Best of all, your dreams are a venue in which God's presence can be discerned. Your dreams are free to express your natural human spirituality even if you are turned off to organized religion.

I believe that God is intimately involved in human healing and growth and directs your natural healing process. At every moment of your life, God issues a specific, tailored-to-fit invitation to become more whole. Whenever you open even a little to God's presence, soon you will be aware of a loving nudge to change, to open up, to surrender more fully, to allow yourself to be a little more like Christ, to become more and more whole.

> **"Paying attention to your dreams is a wonderful way to allow God to communicate with you."**

By wholeness I don't mean hard-body perfection or even necessarily freedom from disease or pain, although I have seen plenty of physical and emotional healing take place through prayer. I mean the unique wholeness that is just right for you now, at this stage of your life. Next week or next year your particular call to wholeness may shift. There is always a next step, no matter how old, wise, or saintly you become. Think about it: wholeness for a fifteen-year-old is quite different from wholeness for a thirty-, fifty-, or seventy-year-old. Even at death—and afterward—wholeness is still available. It's as if God is always saying, "C'mon. C'mon now. You can make it. Just pay attention and cooperate with what I am doing inside you. And don't worry; I'll help you along."

Paying attention to your dreams is a wonderful way to allow God to communicate with you. God seems to like showing up in dreams, often in the oddest ways. Later I will tell you about some funny and profoundly startling disguises God has assumed in the dreams of people I know.

For now, I want to share with you a recent and wonderful dream that I am sure is all about my own current invitation to wholeness. Since beginning work on this book, my own dreams, which have always been important to me, have just bloomed.

## THE FORGOTTEN ATTIC

I am unlocking the door to a building I don't recognize. I know that I purchased this building a long time ago and then forgot about it. I go inside and see modern, bright meeting rooms. I am surprised to find that there is a lot going on in here—music classes, after-school programs, adult education events. Lots of people are chatting and strolling through the rather ordinary-looking halls.

Then I go upstairs and find myself in a dimly lit attic with many trunks and chests lining the walls. I see lots of other objects too: dusty shelves of old books, stacked-up cardboard boxes, a rusty bike, a stuffed owl.

People stream through this large attic as if it were a hallway. Although the first floor is full of life, there is even more energy up here. Excited kids thunder as they run on the old wooden floor, and adults walk briskly along, talking and laughing. Everyone seems to be taking a shortcut through the attic to somewhere else in the building. No one stops or even appears to notice the shelves and chests except for me. I am riveted, fascinated by them.

At first I gleefully imagine filling the storage space. Oh boy, I can keep more stuff! But as I gaze around, my pack-rat impulse quickly fades. I see that some of the chests are old and very fine. One chest in particular captures my attention—actually it is three chests, each about four feet long and five feet high. The three are put together to look like one long piece of furniture. Each chest is a little different in shape so that the three chests form an organic, symmetrical, curvy, graceful, flowing silhouette. Each chest consists of two cabinet doors that are intricately carved and subtly painted. I open one set of doors; behind it are beautifully made drawers, also carved, and painted with lighter colors. I know these chests are valuable, and I wonder how I could have forgotten them. I also know there are treasures in those drawers. In my dream I mutter, "Those appraisers on *Antiques Roadshow* would love this!"

Even though I am asleep, I know that I am in a wonderful and fascinating dream, and I resolve to remember every detail.[1] I am aware that I am encountering parts of myself that I have forgotten and stored away. Suddenly I sense an odd familiarity about this place, and I am excited to be back in this attic at last.

Just as I am about to open a drawer of the three-part chest, I notice another chest to my right. It has glass doors, and I can see violins stored there in open cases. The violins draw my attention. I open the glass door and take out a half-size violin made for a child. It is dusty and obviously has not been played for years. I pluck the strings, and I am astonished to find that the tiny violin is perfectly in tune. (I was a violin major in college.) Even without using the bow, I hear that the violin has a beautiful ringing voice and is much louder than a little fiddle could really be.

As I put the tiny violin under my chin and pick up the teeny bow, the alarm clock goes off. Rats! I don't want to leave my dream. I want to play all the violins, explore all the chests, and find out who all these people are. As I force myself to wake up, I know I want to try to dream about this wonderful attic again.

At this writing, I haven't worked much with this dream, but I can already see that there are treasures to explore, as well as old useless stuff I am still dragging around. When I do work with it, I know there will be surprises, but I'm pretty sure the dream concerns some "antique" parts of myself that I have stored away. I've allowed some things in me to get dusty and forgotten. I am also sure that the dream will invite me to grow in some way, and because I trust my dreams, I know that somehow the time is ripe for this particular new growth.

Best of all, I believe I will discover an invitation from God hidden somewhere in the dream. Where might God appear? in the violins? the people streaming by? the classrooms? the rusty bike? the gorgeous, amazing, oh-so-trinitarian, three-part chest? the dust that covers and penetrates everything? the owl? the modern classrooms on the first floor? the key to the building? the forgetting? the building? something else? I might recognize God's voice as I play any of these parts of my dream, or God might simply be present in this whole dream that so draws me in and prods me to change.

As I continue to write this book, from time to time I will work on this dream, and I will share some of that work with you.

---

1. The awareness that you are dreaming while you are dreaming is called lucid dreaming. This began to happen to me occasionally only after I had worked with my dreams for many years.

# CHAPTER THREE

# CAN'T I JUST LEAVE GOD OUT *of My* DREAMWORK?

C an't I just trust my inborn urgency to grow and not get involved with God or spirituality? The short answer is yes, of course you can, and furthermore I would expect you to benefit greatly from your dreamwork. The longer answer is a bit more complicated, and I must begin with a little background.

The early twentieth century birthed a glory time for science and amazing new inventions. Electric lights flashed on for the first time; automobiles revved up their cranky engines; and newfangled telephones began to ring. Tremendous progress was evident on every front. Scientific thinking was the way to go.

Intoxicated with science and technology, most people of this time regarded dreams as silly and meaningless. Dreams also disturbed the prudish etiquette left over from the Victorian era. Their improbable plots, terrifying images, uncontrolled desires, raging emotions, and even nudity and sex, made dreamers blush in the morning. No wonder people publicly brushed aside dreams as embarrassing foolishness. Surely, though, many were secretly fascinated with their dreams and perhaps whispered to good friends about the bizarre realm they encountered as they slept.

Sigmund Freud's *The Interpretation of Dreams* burst onto this scene in 1913, announcing a new "science of dreams." In his groundbreaking book Freud wrote that dreams have tremendous personal significance for the dreamer, that they reveal hidden aggression and erotic desires (ooh!), that even little children have sexual impulses (gasp!), that dreams are important in treating mental illness, and that dreams can be "analyzed" by a rigorously trained, scientifically oriented doctor. When the dust settled, dreamwork and dreamers were changed forever.

> ❝ Since Freud's time, countless people have learned to pay attention to their dreams and have personally experienced their importance in healing, decision making, self-understanding, and personal growth. ❞

Although few modern psychoanalysts buy into the whole theory put forth in *The Interpretation of Dreams*, Freud's big idea—that dreams reveal vital truths for growth and emotional balance—remains with us. That these truths are not plainly evident but encoded, keeps dreams mysterious and perpetuates widespread fascination with dreams. A second effect of Freud's masterpiece, along with the new scientific mind-set that bloomed about a century ago, is that the religious meaning surrounding dreams became blurred or nearly erased, at least in Western cultures.[1] Dreams, with their monsters and ghosts, their terror and ecstasy, their gods and devils, were now largely the purview of science. In much of recorded history, dreams were viewed as spiritual events and were interpreted by shamans or priests. This is still true in parts of the world; some African and Native American cultures have not lost the conviction that dreamers enter a spiritual realm from which they can glean valuable wisdom. But in the West, dreams and spirituality largely separated. You and I still live with traces of that legacy.

Since Freud's time, countless people have learned to pay attention to their dreams and have personally experienced their importance in healing, decision making, self-understanding, and personal growth. Sleep researchers have also decided that dreams are not just about firing synapses, REM sleep, and alpha brain waves but are an arena for something more. Although they don't yet agree on the exact function of dreams, they are collecting evidence that dreams help us work out various problems, contribute to certain types of learning and memory, and *regulate emotional balance*—just as Freud suggested.

We now know that there are many different ways to work fruitfully and responsibly with dreams, and most of these methods have branched off from Freud to form various schools of psychotherapy. The neo-Freudians, the Jungians, the Adlerians, and, of course, the Gestaltists, have all placed their particular spin on dreamwork.

In addition, many ordinary people are enthralled with dreams, and a jumble of information and misinformation clamors for popular attention. Most large bookstores carry a variety of dream "dictionaries" that often contradict one another but promise to divulge the arcane meanings of dream symbols. A glance at the Internet reveals a plethora of opportunities to have your dreams analyzed online, as well as a widespread impulse to restore spirituality to dreamwork. There is much personal sharing of dreams, idiosyncratic dream theories, and numerous ads from those who combine dreamwork with astrology, tarot cards, crystals, or yoga. By popular demand, spirituality—widely defined—seems to be slowly leaking back into dreamwork.

And why not? As humans we are spiritual to our core. Spirituality actually defines us; anthropologists teach that spirituality is a mark of being human. Spirituality can be found in every culture, in every part of the world, and evidence of spiritual belief goes back thousands of years. Recent development of the "new physics" suggests dimensions of reality that we can't perceive in the usual scientific way, and some cosmologists say that the only thing that makes sense is that the universe is held together by something like what we call God. Is it any wonder, then, that we humans just naturally reach for the stars? We need meaning beyond ourselves like we need water. Even apart from religion, many of us are aware that we are much more than mere flesh and bone. Perhaps you can believe along with me that spirituality is simply innate.

**" As humans we are spiritual to our core. . . . We need meaning beyond ourselves like we need water. "**

Maybe that's why you picked up this book. You may yearn to know the One who created one-celled organisms and petunias, aardvarks and galaxies, not to mention your own amazing self. Maybe you've had powerful "peak" experiences but haven't known what to do with them. Or perhaps you feel that there must be something more to life than the repetitious details and demands you attend to every day. Maybe you catch glimpses of this something more when you respond to love or beauty or when you learn that suffering can be turned into gift. Some people speak of spiritual hunger as a "God-shaped hole" in their deepest selves.

It is possible, however, to ignore even a God-shaped hole. You may not allow yourself to be aware of your spiritual nature, or you may honestly feel that your spiritual impulses aren't that important. Maybe someone injured you by directly attacking your spirituality, or perhaps some group eroded your spirituality by trivializing it or trying to stuff it into an ill-fitting box. As a consequence, you may be a virtual anorexic in the realm of spirit, starving yourself from the spiritual nourishment you need to be a whole person. In my opinion, when you lose your awareness of spirituality, you are missing a vital part of yourself.

I will always remember an old dog from my childhood who lived with my grandmother in the red hills of Alabama. This dog had somehow lost a leg; depending on whom I asked, he "lost it in a coon trap," he was "bit by a rattler," or he was "just born without it." Whatever. Three-Legged Charlie (TLC) was a remarkable dog. Although TLC hobbled badly, he tried hard to keep up with the other dogs. He chased sticks and hunted rabbits; he swam in the river pretty well; he was affectionate with his humans. He seemed determined to make the most of his life and actually did a good job of it. Of all the dogs I liked him best because he was, well, so *valiant*.

You may be like Charlie—you have found a way to manage even though you don't have all your "legs." For many reasons, you may not be ready to claim your spirituality or to look for the presence of God in your dreams or anywhere else. Furthermore, each person's growth is unique, nuanced, multifaceted, and holistic. No two growth trajectories are the same. You and I have differing ethnic heritages, personal histories, patterns of behavior, ways of expressing ourselves and perceiving the world. Just as Jesus treated individuals differently, so the Holy One works within each one personally and individually.

There is simply no way to chart one theory for adult growth, or find one style of prayer, or adopt one sequence of dreamwork that will fit everyone. No one else in the world is just like you.

So, if you aren't willing or ready right now to find God in your dreams, I'm not going to try to persuade you otherwise. You can still explore your dreams and expect to make rich and challenging discoveries about yourself. Determination and hard work can take you, like TLC, very far. Go ahead, and see what happens.

> " If you aren't willing or ready right now to find God in your dreams, I'm not going to try to persuade you otherwise. You can still explore your dreams and expect to make rich and challenging discoveries about yourself. "

In the process of psychotherapy many learn to value their dreams and find valuable direction for their lives, and others find ways to attend to their dreams through books, workshops, and dream groups. I have found secular Gestalt dreamwork in particular to be a simple and extremely effective tool for personal growth, and you certainly don't have to recognize God's presence to get started. Decide later if you want to experiment with letting your dreams and your spiritual hunger get together.

I will explain Gestalt dreamwork in much greater detail in the following chapters, and I will note the additions of Gestalt Pastoral

Care (GPC). For now, know that Gestalt fundamentally trusts dreamers themselves to discover what their dreams are about. Because Gestalt is a nonanalytic approach, no analyst is needed (although you may want to seek out a friend or a professional to be your dreamwork companion). Alone or accompanied, you will need commitment, trust, and a bit of childlike playfulness to find out what your dreams might reveal. Just being willing to explore your dreams is a step toward trusting in something mysterious, something you don't immediately understand.

However, be warned: Gestalt work always invites you to keep expanding your awareness of the present moment. When you start playing around with your dreams and expanding your awareness, you might be startled to discover that God has been there all along. You might experience a holy and loving presence showing up in your very ordinary dreams—in dreamcode. If you are willing to stay open, you may find out, perhaps to your surprise, that this One who loves you is shaping your interior process into a sort of inner curriculum designed just for you, and that this curriculum may wind up inviting you to become more like Jesus. Eventually you might be willing not only to play your dreams but to pray them as well. For many people, maybe for you, faith is born more easily with direct experience than with rational arguments, sermons, or reference to biblical texts. You may find that praying your dreams is a way to feed your spiritual hunger and find your way back to God.

If, on the other hand, you are already a person of faith, you know that all creation reveals God's presence. You have probably experienced God in nature, or in the love of a saintly person, or in reading the Bible, or in the generosity of the poor, or in music or art, or in the hell of a personal crisis, or in your own prayer time, or even in public worship. Probably you will not have too much trouble believing that God could be at work in your dreams as well, even if you don't yet understand just how. You may already sense that it is not so much a matter of inviting God into your dreams but of discovering how God is already at work there.

---

1. Carl Jung (1875–1961), a colleague of Freud, was an important dissenting voice in this regard. Early on in the development of psychoanalysis, he recognized that dreams are partly an expression of spirituality, a venue in which God is sometimes revealed.

# CHAPTER FOUR

# REMEMBERING YOUR DREAMS

### THE VELVETY PURPLE FLOWER

If you don't remember your dreams, you are not alone. Every time I begin a workshop on dreams, someone always says, "I never dream. Or else I don't remember them." Others say they sometimes have a vague sense they have been dreaming, or they may even have a momentary flash memory of a dream. Either way, everything vanishes by the time they are fully awake and pull themselves out of bed.

If you are interested in working with your dreams, obviously this is a problem, but usually a solvable one. Understand that it is highly unlikely that you really don't dream. Not so long ago dream experts told us that everyone enters the altered state of consciousness we call dreaming. Now some sleep scientists postulate that there may be rare cases in which a person doesn't dream. I suggest that for now you assume that you aren't one of those rare people. And even if you are, you can still try some of the suggestions in this chapter for working with dreamlike images of your own choosing.

Typically the problem in dream recall lies in bridging that gap between dream consciousness and normal waking consciousness. You have probably already read some of the following suggestions, since they appear in many books on dreams. I too will name them briefly, because these suggestions really can make a difference. Start with the easy ones first. Toward the end of this chapter I will suggest some additional ways to jump-start your dream memory, ways that may be new to you. For now, just know that nearly everyone who comes to one of my dream workshops finds a way to begin fruitful work with his or her dreams.

> ❝ If you don't remember your dreams, you are not alone. ❞

*First, get enough sleep.* If you are always exhausted, you will find dream recall much more difficult. Waking up after too little sleep, you are so groggy that it's all you can do to stagger into the bathroom and brush your teeth. By then, your dreams have fled. Sometimes, of course, you can't do much about your lack of sleep. When you have a new baby, for example, you will probably just need to accept that you will be a zombie for a while. But even when you must survive a period of deep fatigue, perhaps you can arrange to turn off your alarm and sleep in occasionally. Sleeping until you wake naturally is perhaps the easiest and best thing you can do to help your dream memory. Let yourself come to consciousness slowly and gently. If you want to drop back off before you are fully awake, let it happen. Obviously it is best if you try this when you have nothing pressing to do. A short vacation, a retreat, a real day off, or even just a free morning can do wonders for dream recall.

*When you do wake up, don't immediately leap out of bed.* In fact, don't change your position at all for a minute or two. During that first minute of wakefulness, you have the best chance of bringing your dreams into your normal consciousness. Sometimes you can hold onto a flash memory a little longer if you don't move around. Let yourself replay what memory you have before you begin to stir. Even if you can't remember the whole thing, a dream fragment can be a valuable treasure.

*Record your dream before getting up.* After a minute or two, reach for your dream notebook and pencil that you cleverly placed on your nightstand before you went to sleep. Try not to move around much. Move your body slowly, as if your memory is a container of liquid, and any jerky or rapid movements might cause it to spill. Scribble down some sketchy notes right away so you won't forget the twists of the dream plot. Then write down as much as you can remember. If some details are already going fuzzy, note that too. (A good alternative to a notebook is a recording device. Just make sure it's all set up the night before.)

Sometimes these first three suggestions are all it takes. Once you begin to remember your dreams, you may discover a cumulative pump-priming effect; the more you remember, the more you remember. When you learn to bring your dreams with you into wakefulness, the process happens with more and more ease as time goes on. Eventually you may find that you can hold dream memories longer, even when you don't have the luxury of lingering in bed. You might be able to recall your dreams even on busy days. However, if you are still having trouble, here are some more things to try:

*Eliminate heavy foods and alcohol the evening before you want to remember a dream.* If what you eat or drink weighs you down, makes you sleepy, or blunts your reactions at night, you may find that you are not as sharp the next morning. Marijuana is nearly certain to blank out your dream memory for a while.

*Try sleeping alone occasionally.* When you sleep with a partner, it may be more difficult to wake up at your own pace. You may be more inclined to move around as soon as you wake up. And sexual arousal can quickly melt a dream memory.

*Check with your pharmacist and doctor to see if any medications you are taking might distort your dreams or prevent you from remembering them.* My informal survey revealed that many people, doctors and pharmacists included, are convinced that some prescription drugs interfere with dreaming. The problem is that "dream disturbance or distortion" is unlikely to be listed as an *official* side effect of a particular drug. Pharmaceutical companies, and even your own doctor, may not put too much stock in the importance of dreams, but if your dreams are important to you, why not ask your doctor if she or he has heard other complaints about the medication you are taking? Perhaps a different medication or dosage could make all the difference.

*Minimize stress.* Easier said than done, of course. Stress is an ordinary part of living, and sometimes life hands us tremendous stress, such as serious illness, joblessness, or bereavement. During a crisis, remembering dreams can be downright difficult, if not impossible.

If you are deeply stressed because of a situation you can't control, you probably don't see a way to make your stress magically vanish. But sometimes easing stress can be a matter of cutting back on volunteer commitments, asking for help around the house, giving up trying to be perfect, or taking some time off. Might you be keeping yourself stressed so you won't have to face deeper issues? You are already taking your dreams seriously if you wonder whether your lack of dream recall might be related to the way you are living your life.

See if this statement fits you: "Maybe I really am too stressed. Maybe something has to give if I can't remember my dreams." Also ponder these questions: "Is there something about my life I don't want to face? Is there some part of my life or some memory that scares me?" Or this: "Do I find it hard to put stock in anything that's not rational?" Trust your own hunches enough to record your answers to these questions. Turn your answers over in your mind for a few days. Try praying them too, and see where your process takes you.

*Try talking to your missing dreams and let your dreams talk back.*
This suggestion comes straight from Fritz Perls, the founder of Gestalt
Therapy. He often challenged his students to do this very thing. Set
two chairs facing each other. (Or put two different-colored throw pillows on the floor.) When you sit on one chair, speak as yourself, and
when sitting on the other, speak as your elusive dreams. As you move
from chair to chair, let a conversation develop. If you try this simple
exercise, you may find that your dreams have plenty to say, even when
you have no specific dream memories.

A woman in one of my GPC training classes who couldn't remember even a dream fragment tried talking to her missing dreams.
The experience changed her life. Her brief work, done without input
from anyone in the class, is abbreviated below.

> DREAMS: You don't know anything about me. I want you to listen to me
> for once.
>
> STUDENT: How can I listen to you if I can't remember you? Anyway,
> dreams are silly and frivolous.
>
> DREAMS: Who told you that dreams are frivolous?
>
> STUDENT: . . . Mother! Oh my gosh! She was in control of everything,
> even my dreams. I wasn't supposed to have any feelings at all!

Now, many years later, she looks back on those five minutes of
Gestalt work as "opening the gate to the garden of my inner life." She
reports that this "turning point" introduced her to "the real me" and
marked the beginning of "finally realizing I was a child of God."

Recently I learned the sequel to this long-ago dreamwork. The
night after this woman spoke to her missing dreams, she had a dream
that she easily recalled the next day.

> I am stuck in a mire. I somehow pull myself out, and then I climb over a
> huge brick wall. On the other side of the wall is a beautiful sunny meadow.

She woke up with the astonishing realization that "I just climbed over my mother!" Soon she had a second dream in which her mother appeared wearing a flowered dress and carrying a large bouquet of flowers. Her first reaction upon wakening was, "I don't want any part of her!" but within a short time the invitation to forgive and accept her mother stirred in her. "With God's help, I did it," she said. "And I've kept on growing ever since."

*Just before going to sleep, pray for a healing dream that you will remember in the morning.* Ask that your mind be opened and that the bridge between sleep and waking states be strengthened. Ask God to work with you in your dreams and to be present with you as you sleep. Do your part, of course. Prepare the way by following the suggestions about enough time for sleep, light food, no alcohol, a notebook by your bed, and so on. Keep asking; make it a habit to ask each night. You may be surprised by what happens.

Years ago, a friend of mine offered dream workshops in the sanctuary of a church in Manhattan. Participants would arrive in time to share a light supper. Then my friend would explain briefly how dreams are gifts of God and often are given for our healing. She would tell them about a famous healing temple of Aesculapius in ancient Greece. Sufferers with every kind of infirmity would appear at the temple each night to pray for a dream. Then they would sleep in the temple, waiting for the special dream that would heal them.

Translating that ancient practice into Christian terms, the workshop group would join in Eucharist around the altar. There, like the ancient Greek worshipers, they prayed for healing dreams. In silence they spread out their sleeping bags on the pews and carpet near the altar and expectantly dropped off to sleep. The next day was spent sharing and working with the rich banquet of dreams that inevitably emerged during the night. I look forward to the day when such events might become commonplace in churches!

The next three suggestions involve working with dream images of your own choosing. Many people have found that working on these "fake" dreams helped them recall their own actual dreams later. Meanwhile they engaged in dreamwork that often surprised them with truth.

*Try making up a dream.* Your made-up dream need not be long. Two or three sentences will do, but create a little scenario containing several different elements. Write your dream in the first person, present tense, as if it were happening to you right now. Don't labor over this; just dash something off. Then work with your made-up dream as if it were real. Here are examples of dreams created by individuals who couldn't come up with a real dream:

- I am getting on the train. In front of me is a man carrying a bunch of balloons. We sit down close together, and the balloons keep getting in my face.

- I am working at my computer, and suddenly the screen goes blank. I am pissed off and frustrated. As I try to reboot, a picture of my uncle appears on the screen.

- I am at a meeting at work. I have to go to the bathroom, so I leave the meeting. The only toilet I can find is right in the middle of an empty conference room. There is no lock on the door. I don't know what to do.

Each of these "dreams," created rapidly in a waking state and immediately explored, yielded some remarkably accurate pictures of the "dreamer's" life.

*Borrow someone else's dream.* Really, it's okay. Work on it as if it were your own. When leading a short dream retreat, I often introduce dreamwork by asking everyone to work in small groups using the dream of one person who volunteers to lend it to the group. I find it intriguing to see how differently people respond to the same images. Even more fascinating is that some individuals report significant interior shifts while working with a borrowed dream.

*Choose a painting that attracts you, and treat it like a dream.* Don't just choose a pretty picture, however. Try working with a fine art print that has several images, is a bit complex, and contains nuances of light and dark, murkiness and clarity. Choose art from whatever historical period you want; I have watched people do wonderful inner work with very old art—and also the most modern. I do think some kind of representational art is best, that is, art that suggests a picture of something. However, this is a rule meant to be broken. If a piece of abstract art attracts you, by all means, go ahead and "dream" it.

The idea of using art as a substitute for dreams came from Lydia, a woman who was seeing me privately. This courageous woman was willing to go to extraordinary lengths to heal from the sexual abuse that marred her childhood. Although she sensed the importance of dreams and yearned to do prayerful dreamwork, she had great difficulty recalling any of her dreams. Then one day Lydia came excitedly lugging an enormous book titled *Georgia O'Keeffe: One Hundred Flowers*.[1] As she opened it for the first time in my office, the gorgeous paintings of Georgia O'Keeffe burst from the pages. These passionate, complex, erotic, and sometimes scary paintings became her "dreams" and would be the focus of our work together for over a year.

Georgia O'Keeffe's flowers are never sweet little arrangements of tiny violets or rosebuds in a pretty vase. No, her flowers are huge, often just one flower exploding onto a large canvas. Her amazing paintings look deeply into flower depths, full of bursting aliveness, velvety mystery, pulsating darkness, and searing flames. As Lydia played and prayed various parts of the O'Keeffe flowers as if she had dreamed them, she contacted her strength and fragility, her vitality and her hidden depths, her beauty and her death, the sacredness of her female sexuality, and best of all, the presence of God. Adopting Georgia O'Keeffe as her "dream artist" and speaking as parts of various flowers, she found herself making such statements as:

> I am strong and beautiful and velvety. I'm such dark purple that I'm nearly black. I have folds and creases in my petals, and I bloom with amazing intensity. I'm scared of my darkness and all those folds and creases. . . . I'm not sure I want to go there. . . . I could get hurt in there . . . but I see that my darkness is shiny and lush. I'm surrounded by some smaller bluish-purple flowers and one beautiful green leaf. I am a green leaf, and full of life.
>
> I have a golden center that bursts out of my dark purple, looking like a shining star. There is a lot of energy in my center. That's where God is, in my center. At the core of my center there is a sort of egg. God says, "I am shining in you, lighting up your darkness, your dark purple, and I am guarding the egg in your core."[2]

To me Lydia's work was beautiful, and I was awed by how God was working in her. Five years later she commented,

> I definitely feel different than before we worked with the flowers. I still draw from it, and I'm still assimilating all the changes I felt. It was really important in healing from the sexual abuse. I have some O'Keeffe flower prints hanging in my apartment, and I look at them often to remind myself of the goodness of my femaleness and my sexuality.

Before going on to the next chapters, have a dream in mind, either a dream of your own, one that you've created, a borrowed dream, or an "art dream." With a fresh dream in mind from whatever source, you may find that you will begin working on your dream even as you continue to read.

---

1. *Georgia O'Keeffe: One Hundred Flowers*, ed. Nicholas Callaway (London: Phaidon Press, 1990).

2. See *Black Hollyhock, Blue Larkspur*, 1929, oil on canvas, opposite page 69 in *Georgia O'Keeffe: One Hundred Flowers*.

# CHAPTER FIVE

# DREAMWORK, GESTALT STYLE

## THE TINY VIOLIN

If you are willing to try Gestalt dreamwork, and maybe play and pray with the additions of Gestalt Pastoral Care (GPC), you will need to understand a few essentials. I will start by describing Gestalt dreamwork as taught by Fritz Perls. Then I will tell you what I have added to form GPC. What follows here may challenge your beliefs about dreams. This theory is not difficult, just a little different from other approaches.

## GESTALT DREAMWORK AS TAUGHT BY FRITZ PERLS

*The most basic tenet of Gestalt dreamwork is that every part of your dream is a mirror that reflects you,* even if your dream features a fearsome monster, a beautiful landscape, or your mother. *According to Perls, no matter what, every single icon in your dream is you.* Imagine you dream that you are walking in a desert. The night air is cool and welcoming after the heat of the day. You hear a coyote howling, and soon you see the animal, head thrown back, making a big sad noise. The coyote senses you are near and furtively vanishes into the night. You look down and see a tiny desert flower blooming at your feet, and then you wake up.

In that imaginary dream you are, of course, the one walking in the desert. You are also the coyote, the desert, the night, the welcoming coolness, the howling, the sadness, the furtiveness, and the tenacious, blooming flower. Even the daytime heat, "present" because it is explicitly absent, expresses something knocking around inside you.

Beginners to Gestalt dreamwork sometimes get confused when a dream icon is an actual person they know. They approach the dream as though they are interacting with a real person separate from themselves. But here is the truth: when you dream about another person, whether friend, family, or stranger, *in your dream* that person embodies some part of you. Even if you dream of having hot sex with someone, Perls would say that you are intimately encountering a part of yourself.

Gertrude dreamed that her daughter, Chris, is on a passenger plane flying erratically in great turbulence. Then Chris is jumping, jumping, jumping through space as if on a huge trampoline, but connected to a bungee cord. Then the bungee cord slips off. Once more Chris bounces up an impossible distance, falls toward earth, and finally lands in the branches of a tree. The dream ends in the emergency room with Chris on a gurney, bruised and battered.

Gertrude woke up afraid and upset. Even though Gertrude has advanced training in GPC and knew that Chris in the dream is probably herself, her first reaction was that maybe *Chris herself* was in great danger. Gertrude had worried about Chris for years, and this dream seemed to confirm her worst fears about her daughter.

I asked Gertrude to be Chris in the dream. Gertrude agreed, but at first found it difficult to *be* Chris rather than *talking about* Chris. After a few minutes of getting tenses and pronouns mixed up, she finally said,

I'm bouncing, bouncing, higher and higher. Then, WHEEE! I really sail off, not tethered by anything. I sail high and land in a tree. I'm bruised and banged up, but I think I'm okay. They come from the hospital and put me on a gurney, and I know then that I'm being taken care of. I'm resting. I'm not afraid. I'm comfortable.

I asked her if she was willing to be the gurney and talk to "Chris" lying there. The gurney said,

I will be always be a place of comfort for you, no matter how untethered you get or how high you sail. I give you rest and healing. I protect you and take away your fear.

Gertrude looked up, her face glowing. "Oh my," she said. "I know who is speaking to me now. That's exactly how God talks to me these days. And Chris in the dream is me. Of course she is me. I do bounce around and fly away sometimes, but I am always grounded and taken care of in the end."

## " Dreams are often projections of a part of you that you don't like, are afraid of, or simply don't know about. "

Some people in your dream may be really hard to identify with. If you dream about your abusive father, he is expressing part of you, as hard as that may be to imagine. Perhaps you will discover that you have abusive impulses too, impulses that you need to recognize before you can make peace with your past. Or perhaps you have taken into yourself some of your father's feelings toward you. He may have called you stupid, a pain in the butt, a loser; over the years you swallowed those lies, and at least a part of you believes them. In other words, you now have inside you a "toxic lie" (technically called a damaging *introject*) planted by your father. Such toxic lies are a bit like your cat's hair balls which, from time to time, he so graciously throws up on your carpet. Toxic lies are not a true part of you, nor do they help you, but nevertheless they are present inside you—until you find a way to either get rid of them or "digest" them.

No doubt you have picked up a few toxic lies along the way.[1] As a child you tended to swallow what you were taught by parents, schools, peers, culture, and of course the church. Toxic lies can also grow out of a particular set of circumstances; you may have come to relate to life in a way that reflects, say, your experience of a tragedy or abuse. Toxic lies have a way of being revealed in dreamwork, along with the parts of you that know better. One woman dreamed about wearing a beautiful silk jacket. On the jacket were globs of excrement. Guess which part of her dream pointed to the toxic lie. (The story of this dream is told on page 61.) Letting a wiser, truth-telling part of you duke it out with a toxic lie can make space for wonderful growth. In the next chapter I will show you how.

*Whatever you have disowned in yourself shows up in your dreams. Dreams are often projections of a part of you that you don't like, are afraid of, or simply don't know about.* The personality you were born with was shaped by events you lived through. For instance, if circumstances dictated that you had a lot of responsibility as a child, you may have disowned your playfulness and spontaneity at the same time you acquired a falsely inflated sense of responsibility for the whole world. As an adult you may know yourself as someone who is a rock of responsibility, but you have trouble letting yourself relax, even at a good party. If you grew up in a violent household, or conversely, with a family that was always "nice," you may now be afraid of, or repulsed by, your own healthy anger. If your teachers or schoolmates put you down, you may not know in your bones that you are actually smart and capable. In Gestalt terms, you have disowned parts of yourself. You have put certain parts of yourself into a sealed box labeled "Not Me." Much of the "Not Me" box is in direct conflict with what you believe to be the real "Me."

> " The great gift of dreams is that you can depend on them to be a faithful mirror of the real you, all of you. "

Carl Jung called this disowned material "the shadow." Remember that your shadow does not consist solely of "bad" or "shameful" parts of you. You could also deny good qualities such as your strength, your resilience, your capacity for deeper loving, or your intelligence.

You may claim that you aren't aware of disowning anything, but consider this: the thing about being blind is that you can't see. In the second century BCE, Terence, a psychologically astute Roman playwright, wrote, "Nothing human is foreign to me." Try on Terence's words for a few minutes. See if you can imagine that parts of you could be truly opposite to how you think of yourself. Can you find in yourself both strength and weakness? anger and the desire to forgive? violence and peace? honesty and sneakiness? generosity and greed? capability and ineptness? sin and holiness? Perls called such opposites *polarities*. As you make room for your own polarities, you become more truthful, more whole, and perhaps more open to God's grace.

Another way to discover what you have disowned is to notice what you dislike, judge, or, paradoxically, adore to excess in other people. Then ask yourself if there is some part of you—even a tiny part—that resembles what you find either unacceptable, lofty, or unattainable in others.

I teach GPC in a men's prison, and every week I hear their terrible stories of lives spun tragically awry. There are programs in prison that help the men face the enormity of their crimes, and most of the highly motivated inmates in my class are agonizingly aware of the harm and suffering they have caused. Their challenge is to reclaim the shadow they have disowned: the possibility of being forgiven and a sense of their depth, sensitivity, and innate worth as human beings. On the other hand, I have little trouble knowing that I have innate worth, but the prison environment challenges me to own what I find hard to admit in myself. Trembling, I look into the truth-telling mirror and see my shadow: my own capacity for treachery, dishonesty, and violence.

Accepting, even loving, your shadow can hold enormous potential for growth. The better you know and accept all of yourself, the further you have come toward holistic maturity, or in Christian terms, the more you have become what God created you to be. Knowing I have the capacity for treachery challenges me to love more deeply. Knowing I could be dishonest actually makes me more honest and helps me stop judging others. Facing my own violent impulses, paradoxically, helps me to love more compassionately and to increase my commitment to the way of peace.

One of the best ways to explore your own polarities is to pay attention to your dreams, a realm in which your rational mind shuts up for a while and your fear of yourself does not prevent the truth from being told. When the truths presented by your dreams make you twist with shame, clutch with fear, or shrink in denial, remember that your dreams are all about growing toward wholeness. And you just might discover that the Holy One is still creating you, shaping, molding, inviting you to keep on growing, and gently caressing parts of you that you deny.

You can expect that whatever you have disowned about yourself is present in your dreams, in your own dreamcode. The great gift of dreams is that you can depend on them to be a faithful mirror of the real you, all of you. In the following chapters I will show you a simple way to look into that mirror and see yourself.

*Dreams can bring to awareness your inner growth agenda.* Knowing yourself as you are right now is a wonderful start. But unless you stop yourself, you are always a work in progress. Your dreams can showcase your next steps and invite you forward. For example, as I scrawl in my journal, pretending to be some of the objects in my forgotten attic dream, I get glimmers of God's invitation to grow. Right now I am the attic talking to Tilda.

> ATTIC: I have been here all along, but you forgot about me. I'm dusty and musty, and I have a strong old wooden floor. I hold valuable things that you stored away. I've been waiting for you because you need what is in me, and you don't even know it. I have held all these gifts for you until you were ready to remember me and come back.

> ME: Come back to what?

> ATTIC: You'll find out if you spend some time in here. You know how to do this, so start being the objects in here. Start with the chest of violins.

> CHEST OF VIOLINS: Okay. I hold violins, lots of them. I have glass doors so you can see into me, and all my violin cases are open. Look inside and remember. Remember how you loved to play when you were a child. Remember how it was when you were older and playing in a symphony orchestra, surrounded by music, playing a small part of a magnificent whole, finding out how the notes on your page fit with everyone else's, feeling the sensual thrill of the violin vibrating through your whole body, reveling in the sound textures of other instruments, being swept away by Brahms, Beethoven, Mozart, Bach. Remember playing viola in a string quartet! I'm

holding those memories for you. You have shoved me into an attic and decided that you have no time for me. You think that because you are out of practice, you can't enjoy playing music anymore.

ME: I am attracted to you, for sure, and I hear the passion in what you're saying. I want to see what's in you, chest. I get it: I have violins in my chest. I sort of want to fiddle around (ha, ha), but I don't have time. I'm too busy. I would have to practice a lot to really play again. Anyway, I was never that good. I never got to a true professional level, even when I was practicing hours and hours a day.

CHEST OF VIOLINS: You are so full of crap! If you want to play, find the time. And what does being "that good" have to do with enjoyment? Now hear this: you don't have to be perfect to play! You live your life doing the things you are good at. You've narrowed your focus to what you can do well and have no time for the rest. That is nonsense! You're cutting yourself off not only from a lot of enjoyment but also from the fun of being a beginner again and discovering things for the first time.

Remember the half-size violin in my dream? I was about to play it in the dream just before I woke up. Now the tiny violin pushes into my awareness, so I let it have a voice.

TINY VIOLIN: Well, hello again! I surprised you, didn't I? You thought I would surely be out of tune, with a scratchy, tinny, sound. You thought I might be unstrung with no bridge or sound post. I may be small, but I am perfectly in tune, and I have a big sound. I'm ready to be played, and I'm just waiting for you to pick me up. I am a beginner's violin, sized for a child, and I sound wonderful. So play like a beginner. Be a beginner!

Ah. So my dream is partly about reowning my enjoyment of music, and playing imperfectly just because it's fun. Actually, this part is not so new; for a while I've been longing to play again. What rivets me right now, though, is "Be a beginner." I sense intuitively, dimly, that this invitation from the little violin is much bigger than I know, and applies to many areas of my life. There is something here about being more childlike and new—this may apply to prayer in particular. I don't know how yet, but "Be a beginner" feels important. It's all right with me to let my thoughts stay loose. I invite God to show me how to be a beginner, playing a child's violin with a big sound.

*Your dreams can summarize and anchor new growth that is still fragile.* Dreams don't always bring a challenging message to change; some announce or intensify a change that has already begun. Joan dreamed of finding a pair of glittering red shoes, just like the pair Dorothy wore in *The Wizard of Oz*. Joan takes off her ill-fitting brown sneakers and slides into the wonderful red shoes. They fit perfectly, and now she leaves a trail of sparkles wherever she goes. This dream occurred during a period of rapid growth in which Joan was deeply engaged in claiming her artistic talent, her voice, her strength, and her new delight in being herself. The red shoes were a perfect icon of the important changes already taking place in her.

*Even the plot of your dreams can reveal truth about your life, in dream-code of course.* If you dream that you are lost in the woods, you may actually be "lost in the woods" in your life. If you dream about a speeding, out-of-control car, you may be leading a speedy, out-of-control existence. Someone dreamed about walking a tightrope. Upon awaking, he recognized with a shock that he was indeed leading a precarious life. Always he feared the slightest misstep. Friar Peter, a priest friend who divides his time between leading retreats and giving attention to his own prayer and meditation, dreamed of improvising on his violin with a church music group. The rhythm is tricky, and he has trouble getting in sync with the other musicians. As he woke up, he recognized that his dream plot provided an accurate icon of his life. "My life is all about improvising," he said. "I'm always having to revise my plans when I go on mission. Things change, unexpected situations arise, and I have to respond the best I can. Sometimes it's really hard to keep everything in sync, and my rhythm of work and prayer gets out of balance."

The message of your dream plot is often sharply revealed as you tell your dream or write it down in the first person, present tense. "I am lost in the woods" or "I am lost" sounds and feels quite different from "I dreamed I was lost in the woods." "I am a car, speeding and out of control" might be recognized as the truth about your life. "I dreamed about a car, speeding out of control" is much less immediate and personal. As for me, right now I am a forgotten, dusty attic full of both treasures and junk.

*Your dreams are cast in your own personal dreamcode.* According to Fritz Perls, objects in a dream are given their personal meaning by the dreamer alone; there are no dream symbols with universal meanings. Yes, certain symbols seem to appear often in dreams, but the meaning is unique to each dreamer. You are the one best equipped to discover the messages in your dream, because the meaning of any dream symbol is particular to you. If you dream of a lake, you can bet that your lake will have something different to say than anyone else's dream lake. One person might say as a lake, "I am smooth and serene and beautiful." Another might say, "I am deep and teeming with life." Another person: "There are things lurking inside me that can suck you under." Still another might say, "I am sick to death of people polluting me with their garbage!"

*Dreams are not to be analyzed but explored.* Freud taught the world to approach dreams through psychoanalysis. After telling the dream, the patient was asked to engage in "free association," a process of verbalizing whatever comes to mind, no matter how illogical or crazy-sounding. Then a specially trained doctor would sift through, or analyze, the free associations and the dream itself to decode the dream's meaning, and this interpretation would then be shared with the patient. The idea was that "insight" could cure; when a patient came to understand what her dream meant, the healing process could move ahead. Using analysis, Freud was able to report some remarkable cures.

In contrast, Perls believed analysis to be a dead end, leading not to the truth but to the productions of someone's mind (which are not trusted much *in the realm of dreams*). He felt that all too often, analytical dream interpretation fit the meaning of dreams into previous intellectual expectations. In his iconoclastic way, Perls taught his students that dreams are "a way around the head." He further believed that dreams are not complete until the dreamer *experientially* enters into their reality. He said that awareness of waking reactions to a dream is almost as important as the dream itself, and that the meaning of a dream can be revealed as the dreamer practices some simple exploratory dreamwork techniques.

> " God seems to enjoy showing up in ordinary things. . . . Why *wouldn't* God be present in the process of dreaming as well? "

*Dreams reveal many levels of meaning.* When you work with the same dream more than once, you will probably discover that the symbols acquire nuances and depths of meaning not revealed at first. Furthermore, as you grow, your dream's symbols seem to grow with you. They can take on new meanings when you work on a dream for a long time, or when you return to a dream from an earlier period of your life. In chapter 11 I tell the story of a dream that dramatically changed meanings over time as the dreamer grew.

## THE ADDITIONS OF GPC

Perls insisted that every dream would fit into his theory, and it is true that any dream can be worked on using his framework. It's all you; play the objects and have conversations between them; be open to hearing the truth about yourself as you go along. I have found his nonanalytical approach to dreamwork incredibly empowering in my own life and in the lives of those with whom I work.

However, Perls stops short of my belief that dreams are spiritual events occurring in a realm of mystery and wonder. Long experience has taught me that sometimes dreams reach far beyond psychology. Dreams are not just about me and my shadow but are also a holy venue in which God is present and revealed.

God seems to enjoy showing up in ordinary things: cups of cold water; bread and wine; a baby born to a teenager; the love between two people; "the lilies of the field"; even your own stumblings, imaginings, and longings. Why *wouldn't* God be present in the process of dreaming as well? As you record your dreamwork over time, you may find that you have written your own sacred story, a lifelong story of interaction with the Holy, a story of how your healing and growth have been shaped by God's loving hand.

GPC recognizes that God is naturally present in dreams and in dreamers' lives. In theological terms, dreams are incarnational; they are infused with holiness and a way to know "God-with-us." They show that God is still creating and re-creating everything in the world. Dreams are God speaking your language and gifting you with tailored-to-fit icons that tell you the truth. In chapters 8 and 9, I will show you how to watch for icons of the Holy One in your dreams, and some simple steps for praying your dreams.

---

1. Introjects can also be positive. For example, imagine that when you are young, you learn a family motto that proclaims a genuine, helpful truth. The motto sits inside you, undigested and unintegrated until your adult life brings you a crisis. Then your nearly forgotten motto clicks into place, and you find direction in its wisdom.

# CHAPTER SIX

# FIRST STEPS *in* BREAKING *the* CODE

## THE LUMINOUS CHINESE JACKET

Deborah is a woman of great courage with an unstoppable desire to keep growing. She spent many years in therapy healing from the effects of a narcissistic mother who disregarded her needs and treated her as if she weren't there. One Christmas, completely ignoring Deborah's interests and desires, her mother gave Deborah and her brother identical gifts. Each present came from her brother's wish list.

By the time Deborah entered GPC training, she had healed a great deal, and her mother's sway over her had diminished considerably. She knew herself as a loving, faithful woman of talent, drive, and intelligence. She had learned how to say both yes and no with conviction. Her mature self, as well as traces of her mom's noxious influence, was evident in the dream she brought to her GPC training group. In Gestalt terms, her dream presented a polarity—two parts of her in conflict. (Notice that in her dreamwork her two hands embody the two sides of her polarity.) First, Deborah tells her dream:

> I'm putting on a gorgeous Chinese-style jacket. It is made of beautiful blue silk, and the weave is very fine. My jacket is iridescent, lustrous, luminous, a feast for the eyes. It is simply stunning.
>
> Now I have to release a small fart. I let it go, but to my alarm, my fart turns into diarrhea. A bit of diarrhea gets on my beautiful jacket. I try to

clean it off, but it multiplies everywhere. I am covered with shit, and I am appalled.

I suggest she give the jacket a voice. In other words, I invite her to imagine that the jacket itself could speak. Immediately she says,

> I am a beautiful blue silk Chinese jacket. I am iridescent and luminous. I shine. I am a feast for the eyes. I'm elegant and dazzling!

It's clear to all of us that Deborah has no trouble being the jacket and claiming her shining luminosity. She smiles with delight and pleasure as she introduces us to this wonderful part of herself. But when she allows the diarrhea to reply to the jacket, her mood changes dramatically.

> You think you're so great, but you're full of shit. You can't get rid of me. You're stuck with me forever!

Clenching her right fist, she wells up with tears. I invite her to be aware of her fist. She replies that her threatening, shaking right fist is expressing the shit. Gesturing angrily with her right fist, she speaks even more vehemently:

> Jacket, you just *think* you're beautiful. *I'm* the truth about you. I'm going to smear all over you and make you stink! You will *never* get free of me!

Deborah speaks as the jacket: "I am beautiful, luminous, shining, a feast for the eyes. . . . " Deborah is now manifesting two opposite sides of her polarity, but the sides are not yet in real contact with each other. Yes, the diarrhea is speaking to the jacket, but the jacket is doing a fine job of denying the diarrhea. Silently I marvel at how creatively she managed to hold at bay the diarrhea smearing her beautiful jacket while she developed her inner beauty. When I suggest that the jacket speak directly to the diarrhea, something new emerges.

JACKET (in a loud, angry voice): You, shit, are my mother's legacy. I want out!

Her left hand now gestures vehemently, physically expressing the jacket's truth.

JACKET: No, I want *you* out! I am sick of being kept down! I am sick of you and your put-downs. Whenever you told me you loved me, I knew an emotional kick in the teeth was on its way. You were so intrusive! You even followed me into the bathroom, absolutely ignoring my need for privacy. You were always grinding me down. Get away from me!

Deborah now makes strong pushing motions with both hands and arms. She has cognitively and physically broken the dreamcode: The beautiful and now angry jacket is her real self, and the stinking goo is the toxic mom she still carries around inside her. Now she can drop the dream symbols and deal directly with her mother. Her own body leads the way as she continues to push with her arms. A class member braces up behind a large pillow so Deborah can physically push against her "mother." She pushes with all her strength as she says to her mother,

Leave me alone. Leave me alone! I am sick to death of you smearing me with your shit! Get away from me! Get away, you bitch!

She shoves the mom pillow away. She stops, tired and sweaty, her anger fading. I suggest she tell Jesus what she has just done. She says,

Jesus, I pushed on my mother and told her to go away. I got really angry with her. . . . I even called her a bitch. . . . Jesus, I just wanted to be the girl and woman you created me to be.

She pauses, waiting in silence, eyes closed, and exhaling heavily as if breathing out the rest of her anger and her mother's toxicity. Jesus' response to her prayer comes in the form of an image. In her mind's eye, Deborah, an editor, sees just two magnificent words printed in Times Roman font. The glowing yellow letters shine against a dark background. The words change everything: "YOU ARE!"

With these words lighting up her awareness, she speaks to her mother again, her voice firm and assured:

> *I am* the girl and woman I was created to be! You never loved me. You never even bothered to know me. You just didn't care. The truth is, I'm full of light. I am a beautiful person, full of light. I glow. This is who I really am, full of light.

Then she "hears" Jesus saying to her, "Deborah, you've been closed too long. It's time for you to stand up." Deborah stands and walks around the room, telling us the real truth about herself, repeating what Jesus said. As she speaks to us, she can feel her posture becoming straighter. She is aware of tension draining from her shoulders. She comments that her chest feels more open, as if there is more space inside. We can also observe these changes. She looks taller; her voice sounds deeper. She is, in fact, glowing and luminous.

As the group shares their reactions to her dreamwork, she makes the comment, "I worked hard in therapy for ten years and never got to this place before." I reply that growth is always a process, and that the ten years of work were not lost but made her inner world accessible enough to do this important work.

Of course her growth process will continue. The dazzling Chinese jacket is her personal icon of growth and grace, an icon she will return to again and again as she more fully embraces a new identity that will not depend on ignoring the toxic lies her mother smeared on her but on neutralizing them with truth that sets her free. Then, too, I believe that expressing her anger in depth, her willingness to keep working, and her prayerful faith will enable genuine forgiveness of her mother when the time is right.

Three days after her dreamwork, Deborah phoned to say,

From time to time I can feel that my shoulders want to get into their old turtle-shell position again. Before the retreat, straightening up felt vulnerable and scary, but now it's so much easier to let my body be tall and straight. I feel wonderful—smooth and relaxed and very peaceful. Even a colleague at work noticed the change in me. He commented that I was glowing, so it hasn't worn off yet!

Deborah's dreamwork was purely Gestalt-inspired at first, but when I suggested talking to Jesus, we veered off into GPC. (Fritz Perls would have been aghast.) Her beautiful work was actually quite simple and consistent with the material in this chapter, in which I will tell you how to begin to work and pray with your dreams on your own.

> " Doing your own dreamwork may feel exciting, daunting, and maybe even scary. You can go slowly or stop anytime you want. "

I know that doing your own dreamwork may feel exciting, daunting, and maybe even scary. Remember, you can go slowly or stop anytime you want, and it's really okay not to tuck in all the ends and tie everything up in a pretty bow each time you enter into your dreams. Always keep in mind that your growth is an organic process and will continue throughout your life, if you are willing.

## BEGIN BY EXPLORING THE PLOT OF YOUR DREAM

1. *Decide how you will express and record your dreamwork.* I (and probably you) need a sort of "witness" to the process as it flows. Having a witness means that your dreamwork is noted somewhere other than in your own head. Working with a dreamwork partner or a larger dream group is great when you can arrange it. Inviting other people to witness your dreamwork can be a gift to everyone involved. Your work can stimulate and encourage someone else's. Good Gestalt dreamwork groups are characterized by mutual trust and the commitment to give up analyzing and trying to control the outcome. If you want some supervised practice before launching out on your own, consider working with a professional Gestaltist until you get the hang of Gestalt dreamwork.

If you can't organize a dreamwork group or find a partner, don't worry. Your witness doesn't have to be a person at all. When I am working by myself with my dreams (which is most of the time), my journal is my witness, and of course God is there. First I record my dream in my journal. Then I speak aloud. Speaking aloud, especially when alone, is much different from just going through a mental process. When I actually voice words, I am much less likely to wander off into making a mental list of the groceries I have to pick up for supper. I pray aloud; I tell my dream; I play the parts. I physically move around and allow feelings to come. Often I wait in silence. Throughout, I pause to quickly jot down what is happening. For me, writing does not stop the flow; it helps me stay focused and invites me toward the next step.

If journaling does not feel right for you, find your own way to invite a "witness" to join you. Consider a sketch pad and colored pencils, a digital camera, a video recorder, or an old-fashioned tape recorder. A large mirror can help too, but you still need a way to record your dream so you can work on it when you have time. A record of the subsequent dreamwork is crucial. I am usually surprised at how many important details of my dreamwork I have forgotten even a few weeks later when I review my journal. Keeping a dream record also helps you see the larger picture of where you've been and perhaps the direction you seem to be heading. Occasionally God's leading is evident only when you review, say, a year's worth of entries.

2. *Tell or write down your dream in the first person, present tense,* as if it is happening to you right now. This simple device can quickly clarify your dream's message because suddenly you are not *talking about* your dream; you are *reliving* it. Using the present tense helps immeasurably in bringing your dream from the slippery unreality of dreamland to the immediacy of waking awareness. Relating your dream in present tense offers a better chance that you will be startled by a metaphor that describes your present life. Present tense takes you to your own "present tension" in which you can hear the dream "plot" describe your life in a way that may take you by surprise.

Feel the difference between past tense and present tense as one dreamer introduces her dream to a workshop group. At first she spoke in the past tense:

> In my dream I was wandering around all alone. Everything was covered with snow, so much snow that I couldn't recognize anything. I couldn't hear anything either. It just went on and on, and I never did get anywhere.

She paused, laughing apologetically.

> I'm sorry, this dream isn't very interesting. I shouldn't waste your time. Nothing really happened. I don't see that my dream means much, except that I'm from Minnesota and I've walked around in heavy snow like that.

When she was invited to tell her dream again, this time in the present tense, everything changed as her dream metaphors came alive. Speaking with increasing intensity, she said,

> I'm wandering around in deep snow. I'm all alone. I don't know where I am, and I don't recognize any landmarks. Nothing is familiar except the snow, and the snow just goes on and on. I'm walking alone through nothing. I'm lost in nothingness. I'm afraid I'll never get out.

She began to weep softly.

> I think I really have been kind of wandering around lost for a long time, not getting anywhere. I don't know where I am in my life. I feel that nothingness so often!

In 1967 when I was newly engaged to George McClain, I had a dream that shone a veritable spotlight into my approaching marriage. The dream plot, recorded in the first person, present tense, said it all:

> I am in a small, crowded room. Each of the four walls is hung with George's clothing. A huge pile of his books covers every inch of the floor. I like being in George's space, but there is no room for me in here. I am looking for a place to put my stuff when two opposite walls start to move slowly, inexorably, toward the center of the room. The door is blocked, there is no way out, and I am going to be squished to death!

I woke up sweaty, heart pounding, breathing hard. Immediately I knew that while I loved George with all my heart and wanted more than anything to marry him, I had to keep my own last name. Having my own name suddenly became a symbol of keeping my own identity and not being squished into George's "room." George, who had been very active in the civil rights struggle, was as committed as I to a loving marriage of real equality, and he readily agreed with the message of my dream.

At the time, neither of us knew personally any woman who kept her own name after marriage. It just wasn't done back then, but still we went ahead. As George said with the endearing grin that still turns me into jelly, "If men don't have to change their names when they get married, why should women?" Even now we "keep our own names" as we support each other with space to grow, both together and separately. I still thank God for this dream that so helped shape our marriage.

> " Before you begin working on your dreams, see what happens if you take time to simply notice what is going on right now in the present. "

## PAYING ATTENTION

3. *Stay aware of your reactions as you tell or write your dream. Your waking reactions to your dream—physical, emotional, spiritual, and to some extent, cognitive—are as important as the dream itself.* Go slowly enough that you can really pay attention to what happens as you work with your dream. Keep in mind that paying attention is not a game of "Gotcha" in which you pounce on your foibles and blame yourself for not being a better person; it is just a way to discover what is true as you relive your dream. Let your own organic, unstudied reactions lead you along.

Recall Deborah's dreamwork with "The Luminous Chinese Jacket," recorded earlier in this chapter. Her awareness that her right fist was threatening to cover her with shit forever led her to make a pushing gesture at her shit-dealing mother with her left hand. When she became aware of pushing motions with both arms and hands, she contacted her anger even more deeply, knowing she was being led by her own body (and God working in her inner process) to physically push her mother away. Her prayerful awareness of Jesus' message, "YOU ARE!" was the catalyst that helped her claim her "jacket" more deeply. Her straightened, relaxed, and glowing body as she walked around the room allowed her to believe with her whole being (not just with her mind) that she is indeed a beautiful, glowing person, full of light.

You may need practice to pay detailed attention to your organic process. Before you begin working on your dreams, see what happens if you take time to notice what is going on right now in the present. I suggest that you write down everything you can be aware of for, say, a half hour. You may be surprised at how much you usually miss. Here are some questions that may lead you to pay closer attention:

Is your body tense or relaxed? Where? Are you holding your breath or breathing easily and deeply? Do you hurt somewhere? Are you energized or tired? Where in your body are you hot or cold? Are you physically holding yourself together somehow? How? Are you sitting quietly, or are you moving a bit? What exactly are you doing? Are you rocking, twitching, shrugging, grimacing, drumming your fingers, making sounds, shuffling your feet? Is your hand over your mouth? Are your eyes shut or open?

Do you feel tearful, angry, anxious, afraid, bored, peaceful, nostalgic, numb, jittery? Depressed, curious, drained, joyous? Melancholy, excited, weighed down? If none of these words seems accurate for you right now, find your own words. Where in your body are these feelings located?

Do you have a sense of holy presence, or do you sense nothingness? Do you feel spiritual longing, assurance, thankfulness, anger, emptiness, doubt?

What is going through your mind? a memory? a bit of music? a question? a list of things to do? Are you beating yourself up? Are you working on a problem? worrying? Are you telling yourself an old story of being wronged? Are you remembering someone you love? Are you counting your blessings?

What physical impulses are you aware of? Do you want to stand up? lie down? curl up? pace? get away? eat? dance? stop this exercise? take a shower? Do you stop yourself from following your physical impulses? How do you stop yourself? What muscles are involved in stopping yourself?

Listen to all the sounds around you, and describe them. Describe all the colors you can see and the textures you can touch. Sense the energy of your environment, whether indoors or outside. Is it cozy, stiff, cold, tense, casual, warm, inviting, murky, forbidding, scary? What happens to you as you become aware of your environment's energy?

Notice how you feel after you have spent a half hour on this awareness exercise.

4. *Catch yourself if you are explaining, judging, or changing your reactions; instead, just notice them and let them be.* As you begin to work with a dream, you might be aware that, for example, you are tensing up. Your first responses might be, "Well, what does that mean?" or, "I must be tensing up because of such and such," or, "Tension is not good," or, "I should let go of my tension." Try to simply be attentive to what you are doing at this moment, without any change or explanation.

When you are fully aware of yourself as you are right now and willing to accept yourself as you are, you are poised for change. It might help you to remember that God is at work in your reactions. I am not saying that every feeling that emerges from your dream is an ethereal vision straight from God. Of course not! But honest reactions reveal truth, whether terrible or wonderful. God stands firmly on the side of the truth, and the truth really can set you free. Learning awareness in itself is a wonderful way to cooperate with God's constant creation of you and a way to expand your consciousness of God's activity.

5. *Instead of trying to explain or stifle your waking reactions, try going with them.* By now you know that I don't mean that you should try to make sense of your physical, emotional, or spiritual reactions. Instead, let them be; go deeper into them while you open your brain and body and spirit to allow images, memories, emotions, sensations, prayers, or thoughts to slosh around inside you and spill outside. As best you can, allow your own interior process to sort things out. Don't rush. Let yourself pause to feel and acknowledge what is happening. You might ask, "Does some part of my dream capture my attention? Does the plot strike a chord? Does a memory or a desire surface? Do I feel younger than my actual age? Do my dream metaphors feel true?"

If something reminds you of being five years old, go with the feeling. Give in to it; let it come instead of chasing your feeling away. In other words, deliberately choose to do what you are already doing spontaneously. Close your eyes and allow yourself to be five years old for a few minutes. What do you feel now, as a five-year-old? Where are you? Who is there? Who is not there? What do you need? Tell someone or write it down. If you feel tears coming, don't fight them. Let them fall; in the act (not the thought) of crying you may discover what is making you sad. Are you angry instead? or scared? Stay with whatever surfaces in your awareness. Such discoveries can be enormously healing.

6. *Pay particular attention to your body.* Your own body is a gold mine of information and is important to Gestalt dreamwork, but only if you pay attention to your physical reactions in the present moment. As you tell your dream, ask yourself questions like these: "Where in my body am I keeping my anger, distaste, tears, or fear?" "Where does my breath stop when I take a deep breath?" "Where in my body am I recognizing truth right now?" "Where in my body am I most alive?" "Where do I feel dead?" "Where am I hurting? tense? relaxed? warm?

cold? tingly?" Exaggerate, flow with, what is happening in you. Wait for the dawn of an "aha," a sensing, a connection, a feeling in your bones that tells you, "Here is truth." In dreamwork, you can expect to encounter *many* such "aha" moments.

> **" Your own body is a gold mine of information and is important to Gestalt dreamwork, but only if you pay attention to your physical reactions in the present moment. "**

If you realize that your arms have slightly tensed around you as you tell your dream, go with this sensation. How? Increase your tension just a bit so you can be more aware of it; fold your arms more tightly around your body, and see what happens. What do you notice now? Then pretend that your arms have a voice. Let your arms speak words aloud in the present tense as if they could actually express themselves. You might find yourself saying something like, "I am tightening, holding myself . . . I'm bracing, I'm bracing myself . . . hmm . . . I'm *embracing*, I'm embracing myself . . . protecting myself." Aha! Right there you have made a discovery. Pause to let it sink in. Write it down, or share with your witness. At some point you might let your arms converse with some image in your dream, especially an image that seemed to trigger the tension in your arms.

Imagine that you become aware that your shoulders hurt, and you let them talk. They say, "I hurt, ache. I'm in knots, and I feel so tired.

. . . I'm tired of carrying so much responsibility for everyone and everything. I can't do it anymore. But I don't know how to stop." A dreamer let her shoulders say these words to an icon in one of her dreams: a canary in a cage. The canary replied, "Yes, I'm in a cage too. I'm meant to sing and fly, but I'm cooped up in this cage. I don't get out very often, but when I do, I have a wonderful time. It's time to let me out, let yourself out, let yourself off the hook of being responsible for everyone."

Remember, the "aha" may not come immediately, but simple awareness of your reactions can point you to a starting place for another day. One person said, "When I told my dream, I got helpless and scared. I didn't get beyond that, but I know there is something important in that dream for me. I want to explore it some more."

This dreamer's decision to suspend his dreamwork when he contacted his helplessness and fear illustrates another important point. *You can stop anytime you want, at any point in the process.* Get it right out of your head that stopping is cowardly or counterproductive. Be gentle with yourself. Don't push, unless you sense that just a little gathering of courage is all you need. (And never push, coax, analyze, or otherwise try to control a dreamer who has asked you to witness his dreamwork! Never!) Claiming your right and responsibility to stop or continue when you want gives you control of the process. You don't have to be bullied by the content of your dreams. The process I am showing you is not so much a valiant battle in which you blaze in and grab the dragon by the throat, but one of planting a garden. One day you work at loosening the clods and feeding the soil. Another day you seed and water your small plot. Then you sit in the shade for a while with a glass of iced tea and look forward to the flowers that will bloom in good time.

# GOING FURTHER

## THE RUSTY BIKE AND THE STUFFED OWL

Until now you have just reacted to the overall plot of your dream and paid attention to your reactions. *Now let each object, idea, animal, or person in your dream speak—in the present tense.* Pretend that the bird or the room or the spaceship in your dream can know things, speak, have feelings and a point of view. Then, as best you can, *be the item or person.* In other words, describe yourself as a bird or a room or a spaceship, while continuing to stay as aware as possible. For example, "I am a bird. I can fly and swoop and see the world from above. I sit on tree branches and sing. I have great freedom . . . but I have to eat worms." Pay close attention to your reactions and go along with them.

You might begin with:

- whatever dream image captures your attention

- the first or last thing you mentioned as you told your dream

- the dream image that has stirred up the most feeling

- something that is obviously missing

Perls put much emphasis on the importance of missing items in dreams. If you dream of a house without windows or a person without clothes, play the missing windows or clothes. If you are searching

> **❝ Perls put much emphasis on the importance of missing items in dreams. ❞**

for something in a dream, be the item you are looking for. If your arms seem pinned to your sides, play the role of your missing strength and volition. If you can't decide where to begin, just dive in somewhere. Expect that any of your dream symbols will have gifts to bring to you.

Remember my attic dream in chapter 2? In a corner of the attic is a rusty bike. I don't have much interest or any particular feeling about the bike, and I haven't worked on that part of the dream yet. Let's see what happens if I pretend, just for a few minutes, that the bike is a part of me.

> I am a small, rusty bike. Once I was brand-new and gleaming, the latest and shiniest in bikedom. When I go back to my origins, I am a gift to a child. I am delight and freedom for that kid. I am much loved.
>
> But after a few years, the kid outgrows me, and I am put up here in this attic. I am too good to get thrown out, but now, years later, I'm still rusting away in this attic. I'm so tired of being on the shelf like this. I've been here so long that by now I'm actually vintage, but I could easily be restored, polished up a little, and taken on the road. There is a lot of life left in me. Someone would love to have me. Tilda would love to have me.

Then the bike speaks directly to me:

> Tilda, you need me. I can tell such stories! I can go so fast! I can bring so much freedom! I have a lot of life to give you. You have to get me out of this attic! I don't really belong here. I want to move—I am built to move! I don't want to rust away anymore!

As I sit in silence, I am acutely aware of both the delicious freedom of riding my bike as a child, and my present "rusty" body. For several years now, I have neglected my exercise program. I feel the bike's (my body's) urgent demand to reclaim the freedom of moving, of going fast. Oddly enough, just last week I started again on a daily regimen of walking a fast mile or so. Already I am much faster. I am indeed being shined up and restored. I sit in silence, breathing, absorbing.

Now I recall that a few days ago while I was putting on my sneakers, an older friend said to me, "When you walk, remember those of us who can't walk much anymore. It is a great gift to be able to walk." As I write this, I sense my usual antipathy toward exercise tilting toward faint desire. For most of my adult life, exercise has felt good only when it's over and I can self-righteously check it off my to-do list one more time. Right this minute, though, I actually *want* to walk far and fast.

I feel the exercise imperative coming at me from all directions now and—surprise, surprise—being met by my own desire for moving. . . . I pause to breathe and let this shift have some room. After several minutes, I say to the bike, "I already have taken you out of the attic. Right now I hope you'll be restored. Maybe your rust will come off too." Again I sit in silence, letting the new currents eddy and swirl around. I sense God's presence in the swirling, so I naturally segue into a prayer: "Thank you for this dream, Lord. I want to walk far and fast right now. I really do! Please remind me about my bike when I think I am too busy for exercise. Please grow in me the desire for exercise. Amen." Still sensing God's presence, I feel something happening in my body. The rusty bike/shiny bike icon is—this is hard to describe—very gently and tentatively, being absorbed into my cells almost like an ointment. I sense that desire for exercise could become a real part of me if I am willing to make room for a shift that is still new and quite fragile. . . .

Also in that attic is an old scruffy stuffed owl. I played the role of owl some time ago and recorded the dreamwork in my journal. While my work with the rusty bike invited me to *reclaim* a lost part of myself, the owl prompted me to *let go* of some old baggage.

THE STUFFED OWL: Years ago I had keen eyesight and saw things that other birds couldn't make out. Other birds are beautiful with their color and plumes, but I am just plain brown and drab. For some reason people think I am sort of scary—like a Halloween owl—but I don't feel scary at all. I am lonely. I am wise in an owlish sort of way, and that scares the other birds. I keep asking, "Whoo? Whoo? Who?"

But now in this attic I am long dead. My time is over. I'm all dusty and scruffy, and you have gone on to other things. Really, I have no use anymore. Tilda, you need to get rid of me. Remember me, appreciate me, love me, but for heaven's sake don't keep my corpse around one more day!

As I run out of owl words, I am catapulted into the past. I am a studious, awkward, owlish teenager who greatly prefers Beethoven to Elvis. I am lonely, different, sad, drab brown, and plain. I don't fit in. I can't get my clothes right, I haven't a clue what to say to boys, and I can't make myself get excited about the pep rallies and proms that seem so important to other girls my age. I identify more with the younger teachers than with my peers, and other students in my high school find me a bit scary and weird. I spend lots of time at the library, the music practice room, and church. I am surprised that my adolescent sadness is still so strong. I have been here before over the years and have worked on these issues more than once. Old tears come, and I let them be.

Now I jump ahead to my present age. I am getting a picture taken for this book. Sitting in front of the camera, I am fifteen years old again, self-conscious and unsure. *At the same time* I am joyfully and honestly glad to be who I am right now. It really is time to let go of the corpse.

I feel a letting go in my chest as I breathe in and out. In my mind's eye I see Jesus pick up the stuffed owl and drop it into a trash can. He dusts off his hands with a wink and a grin as if to say, "Good work! I'm tossing out the old pain you've been holding on to. Now love that teenaged kid who was really special. See how I held her apart from the others so I could shape her."

I return to my dream attic. Without the small stuffed owl, the attic seems much larger and lighter. *I* am larger and lighter, and I have more space inside. Yeah!

See how this works? Let each part of your dream have a voice. Pay attention to your own reactions. Follow them out; express them in some way. Take time to allow, to absorb, to deepen your awareness. Wait for the dawn of an "aha!" Remember to breathe as you make room for something new to grow. Share what happens with your "witness." (See p. 66.)

> **" Dream symbols represent various parts of you, parts that may reflect inner polarities. "**

## MAKING CONVERSATION

*Let the images of your dream interact with each other.* Remember that dream symbols represent various parts of you, parts that may reflect inner polarities. Learn to watch for objects or living things in your dreams that seem to be in conflict, or have opposite characteristics, or have different points of view, or are players together in some dream drama. Then play around with the images. If you dream, for instance, that a cat is chasing a mouse, let the mouse and the cat talk to each other. Discover what happens if you physically leap around and hiss as the cat, and cower in a corner emitting mouselike squeaks. Or, imagine you dream of an ordinary yellow pencil lying next to a computer. Such a dream scenario fairly calls out for conversation between the two. The pencil and the computer could also hear from the desk on which both of them are sitting, or from the person they both need in order to accomplish anything at all. Does a teacher from your elementary school pop up in your dream? Have a conversation or an argument with him or her. Be open to discovering how your teacher is an icon for a part of you. Are you in a building? Let parts of the building speak to each other or to you. Almost any object, person, idea, or animal in your dream could relate to any other, and if you give them permission to express themselves, you will probably make some rich discoveries.

Imagine that your dream cat is going to converse with your dream mouse. You will need to find those two very different voices inside yourself and separate them out so that each can have its distinctive say. Gestalt wisdom says you will need two chairs facing each other. (An alternative: I like to do dreamwork with two large pillows while sitting on the floor.) When you sit on chair #1, talk as the cat. When you sit on chair #2, respond as the mouse. *Actually moving your body from chair to chair will help you sink more deeply into the two different voices and keep straight who is who.* (If you find it physically difficult to move from chair to chair, try marking the change from cat to mouse and back again by picking up two different objects in turn. So, for example, when you hold a red throw pillow, you are the cat; a blue pillow in your lap signifies you are the mouse.)

Let the cat and the mouse describe themselves, switching back and forth between the appropriate chairs. Then let a conversation develop between the two. Remember to go slowly, giving yourself time to pay attention and react to what is happening. Also keep in mind that your dream cat and mouse will be different from someone else's, so don't imagine what your average mouse or cat would say. Just speak and let the meanings emerge as you listen to yourself.

Here is the beginning of an imaginary dreamwork dialogue between a cat and a mouse:

CAT: I am slinky and secretive. And powerful . . . but nice. Whatever is going on, I want to be in the middle of it. I wait for something to happen so I can pounce. I like to chase around and then curl up and be real lazy. Whatever I do, I do with all of me. I know you are scared of me, mouse, but actually I just want to play with you.

MOUSE: Play with me? What, are you nuts? You scare me to death. You are big and have big claws. No way am I going to play with you. You'll chew me to pieces. I'm a mouse, after all. The only way to protect myself is to run away and hide in a hole.

The dreamer pauses, sensing an "aha." She repeats what she just said so she can take it in.

The only way to protect myself is to run away and hide in a hole. . . My best defense is running away and hiding in a hole. . . It's true; I'm a mouse. I always run away from anything new and big, and I hole up to protect myself.

The dreamer realizes that she didn't have much trouble identifying with her mouse voice. In the past she has even described herself as a mousy person. She is astonished, then, to hear herself respond as the cat:

CAT: Well, I'm tired of you hiding from everything, letting opportunities to live bigger pass us by. I want to risk loving someone, but you always run away before relationships can develop. I want to travel, but you're too scared. I want to get a new job, but you tremble in a corner. I don't want to hide from my life anymore. Let's get on with it!

The dreamer has now broken the code and unearthed a part of

herself (the bold, adventuresome cat) that she knew almost nothing about. She is face-to-face with a pretty specific inner challenge to grow. Will she? It is her choice. Even if she stops her still-unfinished dreamwork now, she has already gained an important new awareness. Just knowing that there is more to her than mousiness will, in itself, likely bring in some fresh air, which could eventually lead to some shifts in her behavior.

If she continues to work, she can drop the dream symbols and let her familiar mousiness continue the conversation with the emerging woman who is eager to change. This journey could go in many different directions, and there is no road map except her own awareness of what is happening next. If she is a person of faith, she may be able to believe that her very awareness is being shaped by a loving God who is still creating her. Perhaps she will be led to explore a time when she was "chewed to pieces" and ask God to heal that experience. She might discover that her fear was planted in her long ago by warnings from an adult that the world is a dangerous place. She might be willing to invite God to be with her in her mousy hiding place, and see what happens. She might find that her boldness grows strong enough to overshadow her old fearful side. She might discover that keeping herself small is physically painful, and that it feels wonderful to explore the freedom and energy of slinking, pouncing, jumping, and then purring in a relaxed heap. Whatever shape her growth journey takes, almost certainly she will discover that major changes don't often happen overnight but are part of a process of growth.

## WHAT *NOT* TO DO WITH DREAMS: COMMON MISTAKES OF BEGINNERS

In past years when I introduced Gestalt dream theory in a workshop, there were always comments and questions afterward revealing

> **"** According to Perls, analysis is the best way to obscure the message of a dream. **"**

that my listeners didn't fully grasp what I was saying. I have concluded that even though Gestalt dreamwork is simple, it is different from what many already believe, and some may have trouble getting their minds around it. When workshop participants are invited to try Gestalt dreamwork for themselves, inevitable mistakes occur at first. I have learned to end my explanation with a list of "don'ts" to observe when trying out a Gestalt modality.

- Don't tell yourself when you wake up, "It was just a dream," or "This dream isn't very important."

- Don't immediately decide what a dream means before you have explored it.

- Don't ignore parts of your dream that you don't like or understand.

- Don't try to find yourself in a book of dream symbols.

- Don't assume that a dream is a movie of an actual event from the past or a mysterious prediction of something that will happen in the future. In other words, don't scare yourself.

- Don't ask, "Why in the world am I dreaming about broccoli?" (or whatever odd image has found its way into your sleep).

- Don't ask yourself, "What do I think this dream means?" According to Perls, analysis is the best way to obscure the message of a dream.

- Don't forget that other people in your dream are actually you. So the mother who shows up in your dream is not really your mother but the mother who lives inside you, who embodies a part of you—the mother that is a picture of part of you.

So far I have introduced you to Gestalt dreamwork as taught by Fritz Perls. In the next two chapters I will go a step further and show you how to invite or recognize God's presence in your dreams.

# CHAPTER EIGHT

# RECOGNIZING GOD
# *in* YOUR DREAMS

## THE BUNGEE CORD, THE TALKING CAT, AND THE HOLY DUCK

You and I are spiritual beings. The question is not whether or not you are spiritual, but what you are doing with the spiritual impulses you were born with. Something in your core naturally, even instinctively, reaches out for God. Whether or not you acknowledge your spirituality, I believe that sooner or later God will show up in your dreams.

When watching for God, it helps if you obey your second-grade teacher's admonition to sit up straight and pay attention. But even if your mind wanders, and even if you feel uneasy about organized religion, just because you are human your dreams will reflect the natural religious impulse imbedded in you. Maybe this is what nineteenth-century poet Francis Thompson meant when he called God "The Hound of Heaven." God will keep "sniffing you out" whether or not you want to be found, and like a good dog, will keep coming to you in a way you might accept. Believe it: God speaks the language of your inner self and does not hesitate to sneak into your dreams in disguises that might appeal to you personally or at least get your attention.

In the next chapter I will share in detail some ways to recognize and pay attention to God in your own dreams. For now, I invite you to read a few stories of how God has shown up in my dreams and in those of people I know. I have arranged the stories by four types of awareness of God's presence in dreamwork. In some ways these divisions are arbitrary; they are not meant to give the impression that some God-encounters are bigger than others. If you ask me, any encounter with God is pretty big. If you let even one of the stories in this book draw you in just a little, you are on the way to opening up to God in your own dreams.

> " God speaks the language of your inner self and does not hesitate to sneak into your dreams in disguises that might appeal to you personally or at least get your attention. "

1. *Dawning awareness that God is actively shaping your life*

Because dreaming is a lifelong school that challenges you to grow emotionally and spiritually, God's creative work may be revealed as you notice that your growth trajectory is being systematically shaped by a loving hand. Each bit of inner work follows another in a sequence that builds on growth already completed. You realize that you are in a process, a personalized inner curriculum that is taking you somewhere. In retrospect you see that your dreams have shown you what you were ready to face at the time, and as you have worked with your dreams, you have shifted to a new place. Again and again you have discerned truth, and the truth is setting you free.

I once heard Episcopal priest Morton Kelsey say that when he first began to work on his dreams, all he had was an "uninteresting" dream fragment of a peach pit. That was it, just a peach pit. He was surprised to find that he could work on this single image for many months, mining its riches, allowing the message to settle into him. By the time he had finished with the peach pit dream, he was frankly stunned to realize that God was still creating him. He became an advocate of prayerful dreamwork and later wrote extensively about Christian dreamwork from a Jungian point of view.

When Yvette reread her dream journal, only then did she realize just how far she had come. In the one year she had been working intensively on her dreams, she had allowed her hard, protective shell to melt a little, and now she was beginning to risk letting good friends see more deeply into her. Furthermore, her old pessimism was melting; she no longer automatically braced for the worst. Something in her was waking up, becoming softer, more trusting, happier. Paging through her journal, a small surge of gratitude welled up, and Yvette found herself blurting out a prayer: "Thank you . . . thank you . . . thank you." She said later, "That prayer surprised me. I haven't prayed in years, but it just seemed right. I know I couldn't have grown this much all by myself. My thanks just slipped out."

## 2. *Recognizing God's presence as you work with your dream images*

You may discover that God has come to you disguised as part of your dream. God's appearance in dreams is not usually heralded by immediately recognizable symbols such as a cross, a dove, or a burning bush. More commonly God is revealed in the individual icons produced by dreamers, and in the dreamwork that follows. In fact, you probably won't recognize God's voice until you actually work with your dream because God's disguises are so improbable—and so ordinary. When you play each part of your dream, you may unexpectedly discover that one voice is very different from the others, a voice full of love, truth, and challenge.

"You probably won't recognize God's voice until you actually work with your dream because God's disguises are so improbable—and so ordinary."

Of course you could object that you have encountered not God but a good, wise, and strong part of yourself. Certainly that is what Fritz Perls would say. He would insist that every dream icon, without exception, is a part of the dreamer. I disagree. Again and again, dreamers report encountering God in ordinary dream icons. I freely admit these God-stories play best if you are willing to read them with eyes of faith. See what happens if you can muster even a little openness to the idea that God might actually be trying to communicate with you.

The following stories of real dreams highlight God's appearance in some unconventional dream icons. If you are turned off by the traditions and trappings of the church, see how you react to these unusual symbols of God.

THE BUNGEE CORD
A man dreamed he was bungee jumping off a cliff above a river on a warm, sunny day. Familiar with Gestalt dreamwork, he played the various parts of the dream, and, as usual, found that the river, the cliff, and the sunshine all represented parts of himself. He would have

to be crazy, he told us, to go bungee jumping in real life, but when he played himself as bungee jumper, he discovered a daring and trustful man feeling great swooping freedom as he dangled over nothing. To his surprise, the audacious bungee jumper was a part of him, although the idea was going to take some getting used to.

When he began to speak as the bungee cord, however, he knew right away that he was in different territory. He knew he was not describing a part of himself; his own responses of awe, wonder, and tears tipped him off that he was now encountering the voice of the Holy One. The bungee cord said,

> I am firmly attached to you and holding on to you. You can trust my attachment to you because I will never let you go. Yes, I will let you fall, but not too far. I will always provide a way for you to bounce back. I want you to trust me and take the plunge.

## A MOUSE
Another man recognized God's voice speaking in a dream as a mouse who said,

> You don't see me, but I am all over your house. I hide myself deep inside your walls. You see evidence of me everywhere. You know where I've been, and you try to catch me or get rid of me. You can't catch me or get rid of me. I'll always be in your house!

## THE CHAUFFEUR
A woman dreamed she was riding in the passenger seat of her car. Somehow she couldn't quite see the driver. Upon awaking she immediately recognized God's voice when, speaking as the unknown driver, she found herself saying,

> I have always been with you, driving your car all your life. I'll never leave you, even when you want to stop. Even when you can't see me, trust me to take you where you need to go.

## THE KEY TO THE BUS

Jill, a part-time seminary student working toward a master of divinity degree, decided to leave her well-paying job in the newspaper business so she could concentrate fully on her studies. At the time there were a lot of question marks in her life: where to live, how to finance the rest of her education, and where she would be sent after completing seminary. At an Opening to Grace workshop[1] she reported this dream:

> I have agreed to drive a school bus for an unknown friend. The appointed day has come, and I realize that no one has told me whom to pick up, or the route for the bus, or even the name of the town where I am supposed to be going. I don't know where to find the bus either, and most importantly, I can't find the ignition key, although I had it earlier.

After telling her dream to a workshop group, she said with a rueful smile of recognition, "Wow! I'm about to turn my life upside down. You don't suppose that I'm a bit anxious about that, do you?" Then, more seriously, "I know I'm supposed to drive that bus somewhere, but I don't have a road map or the key."

The dream plot presented a remarkably accurate picture of her present existence and how she felt about it. Her body grew more tense as she talked, and she could feel tears welling up. With so many missing elements in the dream, I took a guess and asked her to play the missing key. She agreed. With increasing astonishment and more tears, she heard herself saying:

> I am a key, no, I am *the* key to your new life. Remember that, and don't worry; I'm not really lost: you have just lost sight of me. I control the bus, and you can't go anywhere without me. You have to do the driving, but I will be with you to make the bus go. You don't need a road map as long as you hold on to me. In fact, I am not only the key but the map too. I'll show you how to get there when the time comes.

When I e-mailed Jill six months later, she wrote back, "I'm always misplacing my keys at home, and it can be a great source of frustration when I do. It seems that I was also 'misplacing' Christ by not always keeping my life centered on him. I couldn't get on the right path until I allowed him to be my key."

> " Your belief system, if you have one,
> or the God-symbols you grew up with
> may shape the symbols through
> which God appears. Even so, God
> can surprise. "

## THE HOLY DUCK

The Holy Duck appeared at the end of a long dream in which Julia, a minister, found herself "soaring around in the sky" after getting angry at the way her church was treating her. The duck caught her in its beak and set her down "in a new place." In her dreamwork the duck said to her:

> I love it when you soar. I created you to soar. You don't have to do flips to please others; I just want you to please me. Don't be afraid, because I will always catch you and set you down in a new place.[2]

This dream and her subsequent dreamwork pointed to an entirely new way of being a minister, and later, to a new job. Ten years after having this important dream, Julia still draws strength and guidance from the Holy Duck. Although she enjoys a good fit with her present job as head of an agency that serves the poor, recently she wondered if she was still on track with her ministry. When she prayed she heard the Holy Duck say, "What pleases me is when you are yourself." That small sentence reassured Julia that she was in the right place.

THE SEA

"I am walking alone on a sunny ocean beach," a woman said of her dream, "when I decide to take a swim. I take off my clothes and jump in naked. I love the feel of the cold water on my skin. I am invigorated, alive, joyful, but soon I begin to feel afraid. The sea is so enormous and unpredictable, and I am alone out here. I wake up just as I am swimming to shore."

Later she worked on this dream in her journal. She wrote to the sea:

> You are beautiful, but you scare me. You are so big and so full of nasty things like sucking currents and stinging jellyfish and sharks and tsunamis. I love swimming naked, but I'm scared of being so vulnerable. I'm afraid I might need to be rescued if I mess around with you, even if you are fun.
>
> I'll enjoy you from the beach. You cooled me off nicely, thank you, but that's it for me.

The sea replied:

> Yes, I am more powerful and bigger than you can ever imagine. Without me you could not live; the earth itself could not live. I am the birthplace of life. I want you to swim in me, so I can surround you. I touch every part of you, inside and out. My water is loving, embracing, and I can hold you up. And when it comes time for you to die, I will still love you and surround you.

3. *Hearing God speak directly in the dream itself*

Although still in disguise, God may speak so directly in a dream that there is no mistaking what is happening, even while you are still dreaming. It's as if the dreamwork occurs in the dream itself or immediately afterward. When I was a senior in college, God spoke to me clearly in such a "revelatory" dream.

## THE TALKING CAT

I am in the kitchen of the house in Saginaw, Michigan, where our family lived when I was a teenager. The red Formica table in the breakfast nook, the sink, the stove, even our old dishes, are all vivid and real. I notice that the door to the back porch is slightly ajar, and I walk across the room to shut it. Then I see a small calico cat out on the porch, mewing loudly and trying her best to get in through the door. Her head and one paw are inside, but the door is not open wide enough for her to actually get in.

I am intent on keeping her out. The more she tries to squirm her way in, the more I gently nudge her out with my foot. I don't want to hurt this cat, but no way am I letting a stray cat into the house! I know that once she gets inside, she will just stick around until I give in and let her stay.

Suddenly the cat stops mewing. Motionless, she stares at me, her gaze shooting into me like fire. She says, "Tilda, will you love me with all your heart, mind, soul, and strength?" [See Mark 12:30.] I wake up stunned.

## THE TEACHER, I

A businessman dreams he is alone in an elementary school classroom. He is crammed into a small desk, facing an old-fashioned chalkboard. He can smell the pencil sharpener, feel the desktop, and hear a faint buzz of voices in the classroom next door. He has the odd feeling that this class is special and he is the only student. The teacher strides in, wearing jeans and a plaid shirt. He picks up the chalk and writes just one word on the board in large letters: ARROGANCE. Then the teacher picks up a pointer, taps the board, and says with a smile,

> Your arrogance is destroying your relationships and making you unhappy. You don't know who you are, but I do. I know everything about you, and I still love you. I want to help you change.

## THE TEACHER, II

Dr. Robert Hall is a psychiatrist, a Gestaltist, a devout Buddhist, one of the founders of the Lomi School in the San Francisco area where I trained for a time, and an important mentor of mine. Many years ago he figured large in a dream fragment that changed my life.

I am talking to Robert. We have a long conversation that ends with the following exchange:

ROBERT: By the way, say hello to John.

ME: John who?

ROBERT: John, the fourth chapter!

Still half asleep, I looked up the fourth chapter of the Gospel of John, and I read the story of Jesus' forbidden (by Jewish law) conversation with a Samaritan woman. Read it for yourself if you are interested in the details. Although that story is not explicitly about healing, at 3:00 a.m. I was swept with an urgency to explore the Christian ministry of healing. The whole incident turned me off and scared me to death, and I stalled for more than a year before really working on this dream. In retrospect, I believe that Robert's dream comments were the opening salvo in an increasingly insistent call to healing ministry.

## THE SHED THAT MORPHED

Years later I had another dream that I believe presented a specific summons from God. An invitation to make my dream come true was in the breathless excitement and conviction I felt as soon as I woke up. This conviction persisted for several years until finally, finally, the dream became reality.

I am using a brush and roller to paint the interior and exterior of a shed. The shed is small with a steeply slanted roof and is set in the woods. As I paint, the shed gradually morphs into a tiny chapel. In vivid detail I see a rug on the floor, along with a fabric-covered mattress and pillows for sitting. A large window in the highest wall looks out into a birch grove. In the window hangs a rustic cross made of two birch branches. A smaller window across from the door opens for ventilation. A low table under the large window is covered with a handwoven cloth. A chalice and plate are placed in the center of the table, along with a small vase of wildflowers.

I knew right away that I needed to build this chapel and do the construction myself. But how? I had never even made a birdhouse, much less a small building. We didn't have the money either, even for materials. So the chapel dream simmered for a few years until one day a colleague named Lowell Johnson heard me mention the dream. "I'll help you," Lowell said immediately. "I'd love to!" At the time I didn't realize that he was a good amateur carpenter. He just happened to be looking for another project, he said, and he would teach me what to do as we went along.

Lowell's first move was to cruise around Staten Island looking for construction sites, because he knew that tons of good building materials are thrown into Dumpsters every day. With the tacit approval of various construction crews, he picked up most of what we needed for free. About that time I received a small inheritance from a relative that just covered the cost of a new door and two good windows, one large and one small.

The next summer Lowell and I built the little chapel behind the house in the Poconos that my husband and I own. It is still there in a birch grove, looking very much like it did in my dream. An added gift came from my good friend Gail Metzger, who made a beautiful circular stained-glass window of a descending dove. Rich Crockett, another friend, made a frame, and he and Gail installed the dove just above the large window.

The chapel exudes a special peace and silence. Every time I go in, I am slowed and stilled. Over the years it has become an anchor of interior rest and renewal, a place of gratitude and blessing. Many others also use the chapel for private prayer and meditation. (It can hold three people if they are good enough friends to sit close together. Most use the chapel alone.) A notebook in which visitors write comments attests that the chapel has been a great gift for them as well.

## A REFUGEE CHILD

A woman who has prayed regularly for many years dreams about a refugee camp. She finds herself near a child lying limply on a pile of dirty rags, his emaciated and naked body covered with sores and flies. She sits down beside him and weeps and weeps. As she dries her tears, she feels oddly refreshed.

In her dreamwork, she tried playing the child, but no matter how hard she tried, the child just didn't seem to connect with her own being. Her tears began again, and she gave in to them, letting herself cry for the child and others like him. Again she was energized when her sobs ebbed away. Still puzzled, she prayed for the truth of this dream to surface. Then she heard God say in her "mind's ear":

> I have given you my tears to cry for the pain of this child and for all suffering children. I am this suffering child. I want you to learn to pray this way. I do not ask you to bear the pain but to share it with me for a little while.

As she reflected on this experience, she sensed she was in the presence of a great mystery, and that her sense of relief and refreshment, and yes, joy, confirmed that she had heard rightly. She still counts it a great privilege to be invited from time to time to pray in this special way.

4. *God appearing in a dream disguised as a traditional or biblical symbol such as light, fire, an angel, or a cross*

I believe that instances of God appearing in a dream disguised as a traditional or biblical symbol are rare, but they do happen, as the following stories illustrate. Such stunning clarity is a great gift.

## JESUS AND THE PEACE BALL

Alexandra MacCracken had an extraordinary dream, woke up for a while, went back to sleep, and had a second dream. Later that morning she did some intensive dreamwork. Talk about being in school! She tells her first dream:

> I don't know where I am, but I know that I am praying. I am feeling shaky and unsure of myself. My life is full of tension and pain and demands and unresolved issues, and I just don't see the way forward. Then Jesus appears in front of me. He is carrying a large lighted ball. He hands it to me, saying, "My peace I give to you."
>
> I am overwhelmed. I take the ball and hug it to myself. The ball disappears into my body. Although I can no longer see the ball, I feel such peace inside. I wake up amazed and marvelously peaceful.
>
> I feel wonderful for a while, but my peace doesn't last. My old habit of flogging myself kicks in, and soon my old self-doubt returns. I begin to wonder if the dream is really from God. And then I beat myself up for not hanging on to a gift God was trying to give me.

Now she talks about her second dream:

## THE SAGGING FLOOR

> I am in an old Roman house with marble floors and a large central atrium surrounded by little alcoves. Somehow I know that one of the little alcoves opening onto the atrium is for me to live in. There is some furniture there already, but I ask some friends to help me move my stuff in. It is a wonderful space, but as soon as we get inside my alcove, we discover that the beautiful rug is sagging in the middle. We see that there is a sort of depression in the floor itself, like something extremely heavy is pulling the floor downward. I wake up feeling my familiar tension.

I ask Alexandra if she would play the floor. She says:

> I am a floor covered by a pretty rug, but I am sagging in the middle. Something very heavy is pulling me under. There is a heavy weight attached to me underneath, distorting me, sucking my energy.

I ask if she is willing to go under the floor and investigate. Again Alexandra agrees, closes her eyes, and says:

> I am in the basement, which is in good repair. I see a huge rusty vat suspended from the ceiling pulling down the floor above. The vat is full of sludge. I know it is my self-doubt, anxiety, and pain. It is very heavy.

I suggest that she invite the Jesus of the glowing ball to join her there in the basement in front of the vat of sludge. She readily agrees and closes her eyes.

> Jesus is coming down the stairs. . . . He is unbolting the vat from the ceiling. It drops to the floor of the basement. . . . He comes over to me and puts his arm around my shoulder. I feel that peace that I felt before.

Together we prayed that the peace that passes understanding, the peace that can cause a vat of sludge to fall on the floor, would find a home inside her. We prayed that Christ's peace would especially touch her self-doubt, anxiety, and pain.

A few months later, Alexandra reflected on her two dreams. "I'm in a much better place since that dreamwork," she said. "The peace has really gotten assimilated, and I know I'm still in some kind of transition to something even better. I'm very grateful to God."

Obviously, your belief system, if you have one, or the God-symbols you grew up with may shape the symbols through which God appears. Even so, God can surprise. I once had a dream that featured Tibetan Buddhist prayer flags. I didn't know anything about prayer flags until I did a bit of research.

A friend of mine had a long, involved dream about the sphinx. She discovered that the sphinx represented immortality in ancient Egypt only after her own dreamwork revealed that her dream sphinx was an icon of the eternal God.

Then there is the dream of a Jewish woman with life-threatening heart disease. She told her dream to a workshop group one evening:

## A NEW HEART

Somehow I can see inside my body, and I look at my own heart. It is small, scrunched up, pale and weak. When I see my piss-poor heart, I am fearful and worried.

I look up and see Jesus in front of me. He looks like one of those awful garish Roman Catholic pictures of Jesus pointing to his own exposed heart. I am not just seeing a picture, though. It's him, all right, although I have to say that for a Jew, he looks extremely goyish. What completely repulses me, though, is his open chest dripping with blood. Yuck!

Then Jesus says to me, "I am putting a new heart in you." I wake up blown away and crying.

With tears flowing again, she blurted out, "I *hate* this dream, but I know it's important. I don't have any idea what to do with Jesus or what this dream means. I hope it means healing somehow, but I'm *Jewish,* for chrissake!" Then her gaze swept the room full of Christian clergy and laity, "How would you people like it," she said, "if you were visited in a dream by . . . uh . . . uh . . . ZEUS?"

I asked her if she was willing to work on this dream, even though she was so turned off by the Jesus image. She said, "I came to this *Christian*"—she rolled her eyes—"retreat precisely to address this dream. Why else would I be here? Of course I want to work on it!" Her remarkable dreamwork took the better part of an hour, and for most of that time she was having a big argument with Jesus. To their credit, the workshop participants gave her freedom to do her work without interruption. I have greatly condensed the conversation but kept the general flow.

JEWISH WOMAN: Jesus, what the hell are you doing in my dream? You look terrible! If you decide to weasel into my life, at least don't show up looking like really bad art.

JESUS: I will come in the way you most need.

JEWISH WOMAN: Oh, don't give me that crap! You pop up in my dream and scare the shit out of me. Then you dangle the idea of healing. What, are you trying to make me crazy?

(Jesus is silent.)

JEWISH WOMAN: Well? Well? Are you going to heal me or not?

(Jesus is silent.)

JEWISH WOMAN: Oh, just great! Now you won't talk. Okay. You don't talk to me, I don't talk to you.

(Jesus, the woman, and everyone else is silent.)

JEWISH WOMAN: I can't really believe you are going to heal me, if that's what you're after. . . . How can I believe it? I just don't believe in fairy stories. But how can I blow you off if there is a chance you might really . . . uh, do something?

(More silence.)

JEWISH WOMAN: Okay, okay. I'll play your game. If you're gonna heal me, you can come any way you want. Come as a damn poodle, if it strikes your fancy. Whatever.

JESUS: Will you let me put a new heart into you?

JEWISH WOMAN (tense shoulders letting go, eyes welling up): Oh . . . that would be just . . . extraordinary.

In her mind's eye she saw Jesus reach out toward her. She physically felt Jesus lightly touch her chest. At that touch, she felt a burning, tingling sensation in her heart. Her breath deepened, her pale face flushed, her trembling body relaxed. A beautiful smile played on her face. "I don't know what just happened," she said, "and I can't begin to make sense of it, but I feel a jolt of new energy. At the same time, I feel just incredibly peaceful."

The retreat group was silent, in prayerful awe of the sheer holiness of what was occurring, letting the woman have time to breathe. The truth is, none of us could have spoken at that moment. There was no space in the room for theologizing, preaching, commenting, or quoting scripture. It was as if we were hushed up by something outside ourselves and left with almost no ability to speak. One by one we drifted off to bed.

By the next morning someone had looked up *heart* in a concordance and shared with us the scripture Jesus referred to: "A new heart I will give you, and a new spirit I will put within you; and I will remove from your body the heart of stone and give you a heart of flesh" (Ezekiel 36:26). The Jewish woman had not known that Jesus had alluded to scripture in her dream, but she speculated that she had probably heard the scripture somewhere. "But," she added, "this verse was certainly not part of my conscious vocabulary."

Still, no one had much to say to her except that we were awed by her experience. Of course we spoke briefly about our odd "silencing" and how we just didn't know what to make of it. Finally all we could say was that it just didn't seem right to butt in.

The woman replied,

> I'm really grateful you didn't start preaching at me. I would have clammed right up. I hope I didn't offend anyone by what I said. . . .

We shook our heads, and someone said, "Your honesty taught me something about prayer. Thank you." The Jewish woman continued,

> I really appreciate that in this group it seemed okay to just come out with whatever I was feeling. I don't know if I just talked myself into an experience, or what. I have a lot to process about Jesus and that touch, and believe me, I will. I guess I'll find out more when I next meet with my cardiologist. But I have to say that I feel better today than I have for years.

Each time I tell this story everyone asks, "Well, what happened in the end? Was she really healed? Did she convert to Christianity?" Sorry, I just don't know. The woman didn't contact me after the workshop, nor did I contact her. Ordinarily I would not hesitate to follow up after a workshop, but whenever I thought about giving her a call, I had that same funny feeling of being silenced. After a while I sensed that the workshop group had been used to witness this woman's journey for a weekend, and now our part was over. Eventually I let go of my curiosity to know the sequel of an already pretty spectacular healing story.

---

1. Opening to Grace is an intensive weekend-long healing retreat based on the principles of Gestalt Pastoral Care. With just six participants and a few observers/intercessors, each person has the spaciousness to decide whether to explore her or his depths—or not. I have come to expect that most participants will be deeply touched, and some will take important steps in the healing of long-standing emotional or spiritual pain. For more information, visit the Web site www.gestaltpastoralcare.com.

2. The complete story of "The Holy Duck" dream is told in *Consenting to Grace* under the subtitle "The Flipping Minister." See pages 210–13. This book is available at www.gestoralpastoralcare.com.

# PRAYING *Your* DREAMS

I've been slowly learning how to pray my own dreams for many years, and I'm still in the dream-praying elementary school. Part of this schooling has been to teach others, either in one-on-one settings or dreamwork retreats, what I've learned so far about praying dreams. Of one thing I am certain: the following suggestions "work," not as a surefire method to get God to put in an appearance but as guidelines to open yourself to what God might be up to in your life. Which leads me to the first suggestion.

1. *Give yourself permission to be powerless.* Tell yourself out loud (really!) or in your journal (actually write it out) that when it comes to God's activity, you can't *make* anything happen. Prayer is not magic, nor is it about gaining control or becoming a spiritual master. Praying your dreams has to do with opening, paying attention, recognizing, and consenting, all of which you will do imperfectly. Imperfect prayers are the best kind because they are honest. Of course you can pray the beautiful, well-worn prayers of the church if you want, but I suggest you spend at least a little time finding your own prayers, even if they seem awkward.

2. *Give yourself permission (aloud or written) to be simple and transparent.* Tell yourself that it's okay to fumble around and search for words or even run out of words altogether. Silence, awareness, and breath can be a wonderful way to pray.

So can noise and storm. Remind yourself that God is big enough to deal with whatever is skulking around inside of you. Why put on a show if God has been there for the rehearsals and already knows how you feel about your lines? Permit yourself to express anger if you indeed are angry. Say out loud how turned off you are to the whole prayer business, and that you don't believe that anything will come of it, if that's what you feel. Tell God if you feel deadened to yourself or to spirituality. One of the most genuine prayers I ever heard began with "Dammit! Dammit! Dammit!"

Take a trip through the Psalms and discover just how emotionally and spiritually raw real prayer can be. Also read in the Psalms how deep is human longing for God, and how joyful it is to surrender to the One who loves you. You might start with Psalm 10 or 13 and go from there. You will notice that many psalms flip with lightning speed from the psalmist pulling out his or her hair to expressing serene, rock-solid faith. I read these "flipping" psalms either as summaries of someone's spiritual journey that developed over time, or as ancient permission slips for me to be really honest in my own prayer. "Go ahead," the psalmists seem to say, "it's okay to pray your rage, your doubt, your despair, and your faith all together in one muddle."

> " Take a trip through the Psalms and discover just how emotionally and spiritually raw real prayer can be. "

One caveat: sometimes your prayer will naturally be full of drama, but if you try for drama instead of transparency, soon you will just be talking to the walls. You will need to go deep, be really honest, and engage as fully as you can with your deepest self. Your dreams can be of immeasurable help in being honest with yourself and with God. You might be able to edit your speech or even your thoughts and feelings, but you will find it difficult to edit your dreams. Remember, your dreams aren't bound by your "shoulds" and "oughts"; instead they offer the gift of truth—if only you are willing to pay attention.

3. *Pray for openness to be alive to God's presence.* If praying for openness seems contradictory when you are angry, doubting, or deadened, well, so what? Which rule book dictates that you have to feel only one emotion at a time? Let's assume that at least a tiny part of you wants to be open to God, or you wouldn't be reading this book. Or that you really long to be open, but you just can't. You want to trust, but you don't. Right there is the point. You and I can't fully open our whole hearts to God without God's help. So ask to perceive how God may be communicating with you. Ask to recognize truth when it hits you in the face. Ask that your mind's eye be opened so you can see. While you are at it, ask about your mind's ear, your mind's heart, and your heart's mind.

4. *Pray the plot of your dream.* Tell the dream plot to God using the first person, present tense. Remember that you are speaking in metaphors!

So, for example, you might find yourself praying, "God, I'm lost in the woods. I am looking for a path, but I don't see one anywhere." Or, "Holy One, wherever you are, I want to tell you that I am finding a room in my house that I didn't know was there. I am really curious about my new room." Or, "Jesus, I'm on a boat in the river. The current is getting stronger, and I can't control the boat. I'm so scared that I'll get swept away." Or, "Creator of the Universe, I am having sex with someone I don't even know! Whoo! I am incredibly alive right now, really turned on. At the same time I'm incredibly afraid."

As best you can, stop talking (even in your head) and let what you have just prayed hang in the air. Feel into your reaction, and pray that too: "God, I really am lost right now. I just don't know how to find my way out of the mess I'm in." Or, "What am I gonna do with all this dream sex? Which two parts of me are coming together? Please show me what I'm afraid of."

> ❝A close relative of dreaming is imagining, and God sometimes chooses both waking imagination and dreams to communicate with us.❞

Remember the lost woman from Minnesota who dreamed about the endless snow (p. 67)? When she prayed her dream plot, she repeated her dreamwork statement as prayer: "Holy One, I think I really have been kinda wandering around lost for a long time, not getting anywhere. I don't know where I am in my life. I feel that nothingness so often!" God's reply formed in her mind: "I am in the snow with you. I am in your nothingness." As she let that idea soak in, a snippet of the Twenty-third Psalm surfaced in her awareness: "He makes me lie down in green pastures; he leads me beside still waters; he restores my soul" (vv. 2-3). These verses, which she'd memorized as a child, now prompted her to pray, "God, I am so tired of being iced in. Please lead me out of this snow. Take me to green pastures and still waters." Then it was as if God, in the form of an angel, appeared in her memory of the snowy dream and, gently touching her elbow, led her to a small pond in a summer meadow. Invited to sit on the grass, she sensed that she had been brought to a special place of healing and restoration. Her part was simply to rest there a while. Weeping gently, she felt layers of tension slide off her body as she breathed in the fragrant air. A few months later she said, "Sitting by that pond with the angel, I felt my energy and interest in life returning. I have not felt so alive and so un-lost for a long time. Sometimes I still go back there to sit some more. I know that I'm not yet through with whatever God is healing."

5. *Experiment with faith imagination.* A close relative of dreaming is imagining, and God sometimes chooses both waking imagination and dreams to communicate with us. The woman who was led by an angel out of snowy nothingness into summer warmth is a wonderful example of what can happen when you put your imagination on the same plate with your dreams and your spirituality. The result is a rich feast indeed.

Faith imagination is a way of praying in which you give God access to your imagination, inviting the Holy One into whatever situation needs healing or clarity. You might invite God to be with you before you even start to work on your dream, and then open your imagination to perceive how God will respond. In other words, allow yourself to imagine God's activity, remembering that God can and often does shape your awareness. Pay close attention to what happens next, and try not to edit the results. You may be aware of images, intuitive sensing, physical sensations, desires, impulses, songs, memories, words that seem to show up in your "mind's ear."

Teaching faith imagination prayer is a staple of my healing ministry. I have found that God touches many needs through access to pray-ers' imaginations. Gestalt dreamwork provides a fertile context for faith imagination prayer. When you reexperience (rather than just think about) a dream, you actively imagine your dream and encounter your tailored-to-fit dream symbols. As you invite God to enter into your dream, your imagination is already in high gear and perhaps ready to welcome God in whatever guise God chooses to appear.

Before you try faith imagination, keep in mind that different people imagine differently, using four basic modes of perceiving that combine in various ways. Most people think that imagination is a process of seeing images in your mind. Actually, your imagination can be nuanced and vivid without any images at all. True, the majority of people imagine visually. If those with a *visual* perceptual preference are asked to visit imaginatively their third-grade schoolroom, they are likely to report visual images: the cracked blackboard, the little wooden desks, the gerbil cage in the corner.

In contrast, *auditory* people may not "see" anything much, but they will "hear" the squeak of the chalk on the blackboard, or the whispering of the unruly kids in the back, or the class droning the multiplication tables.

*Sensate* people may not "hear" or "see" anything except in a fuzzy way. Their imagining takes the form of experiencing the classroom in their bodies. So, they might feel the smoothness of the wooden desk or the familiar stomach-clutching fear when the teacher calls on them.

Finally, *cognitive* people primarily imagine with thoughts. They might report something like, "In my third-grade classroom I finally figure out that real learning is putting facts together into new patterns. I realize that I am waking up to a new way of being alive."

Try to identify your own preferred way of imagining by going back to your own childhood classroom. You will probably put one or more of these modalities together so that your experience is, for example, visual-auditory or auditory-sensate. Maybe you even experience all four modalities together. The point is to welcome the way your imagination works and let it do what it wants.

In faith imagination prayer, let your capacity for imagining have some room. Give it some freedom. Put another way, do your best to trust that God is shaping both your capacity for imaginative thought and your attention. You can, and should, evaluate your experience later. But for now, take your foot off the brake, and don't stall your imagination even before you let it take a trip. After all, your dreams are already taking you on trips that can be beautiful, scary, improbable, and usually surprising. So as you pray for openness, for example, throw out your ideas about just what form God should take. Imagine the Holy One near you. For now, be open to what plays in your imagination. Have enough trust to write down your experience and see what happens.

I know someone who says that imagining God's presence is like sensing that someone has sneaked into the room behind her. Another person sometimes sees words of scripture in his mind's eye. More rarely he "hears" words spoken in a silent voice. A third says that when he opens his imagination, he sees Jesus, often dressed in jeans, gesturing, beckoning, and sometimes touching him. Yet another feels her body relax as if it is "absorbing the Peace surrounding her."

All of these people, well experienced in prayer, sometimes feel absolutely nothing when they pray. When they try, all their usual ways of opening to God go nowhere. All their familiar routes have barriers with big signs that say "Road Closed." I can almost guarantee you will sometimes feel a lot of nothing when you try to pray. You are sure that no one is listening and that you are fooling yourself. Other days you may be so jumpy and distracted you can't sit still, much less open your heart and imagination to God. At these times it might help to remind yourself that God knows your desire to pray, and your longing itself is actually a prayer. Also remind yourself that your prayer is not a summons; God will not be controlled. Try again—and again.

6. *Invite the Holy One to enter your dream plot in your imagination.* The Minnesota woman in the snowy dream prayed in this way. So did the woman who dreamed of the vat of sludge pulling down her floor. You might pray, for example, "Please come into the woods and help me find the path." Or, "Please come into my house and into this new

room and show me what's here. What am I supposed to see? . . . What do you want me to do with this room?"

As you are praying, pause frequently. Wait. Breathe. Be in silence, letting God have access to your imagination, your feelings, your body, your mind. Pay attention to what happens next. Don't be afraid to allow your dream to develop a new ending; this often happens when praying with faith imagination in the context of dreamwork. For example, check out the story on page 126 of the man who had a nightmare of falling through limitless space but never landing.

7. *As you play the various images and objects in your dream, pray them too.* You can do much more than pray your dream plot. Each part of your dream contains a truth. As you play each part, tell the Holy One what you are discovering. Again, wait for a response. Ask that if you are not getting it right, God will help you to a more truthful place. As always, pay close attention to hunches, shifts in awareness, emerging memories, and especially to your own body. Wait some more and stay with what is happening to you. Tell God how you are reacting. When you let the various parts converse and more is revealed, pray that too, and open yourself to God's response.

8. *When you work with your dream, be alert for a dream icon that may symbolize the Holy One.* Obviously you don't want to jump to conclusions or make up anything. However, those who pray their dreams find that again and again they are surprised at what they find themselves saying. So play the various parts of your dream with a waiting heart. Pray that you recognize the moment when a person or object in your dream reflects the voice of God. Wait for the thud of recognition in which some pieces inside of you rearrange themselves into a new pattern. Pay particular attention when your stomach, your shoulders, or your back knows you have met a truth much bigger than you. You let out your breath, and you realize you just let go of something besides air. You inhale, and what comes into you is holi-

ness, peace, acceptance, excitement. Perhaps you are stilled, slowed, gulping, set back into yourself, awed by Presence. Or perhaps you simply have a sense of knowing that you've been addressed. Maybe there is a rightness about your experience that convinces you. Maybe this is what Jesus was talking about when he commented that sheep recognize the shepherd's voice (see John 10:1-5).

> **"Especially if you are having trouble with churchy words and traditional symbols, a dream icon of the Holy might help you open the door just a crack to let God in. "**

Once you have identified a dream icon that mediates God for you, try focusing on that icon as you pray. Your icon is a great gift— a tailored-to-fit symbol of the Holy One that appears at a particular time in your life. Especially if you are having trouble with churchy words and traditional symbols, a dream icon of the Holy may help you open the door just a crack to let God in. God seems to enjoy morphing into something small enough for us to perceive at a particular time and place. The woman who dreamed "The Holy Duck" (p. 91) now, years later, occasionally returns to that compelling image as she prays. I don't mean to imply that you adopt a certain dream symbol as your only icon of God's presence. No one symbol can point to the hugeness of God. Perhaps eventually you will be ready to embrace several symbols—some deeply personal, some collective.

9. *If you don't perceive any flicker of God's presence as you work on your dream, specifically invite God to come in.* Return to your dream when you are awake. Enter it and reexperience the dream as vividly as possible. Then invite the Holy One to come into your dream with you. Pay close attention to what happens. In other words, practice faith imagination using your dream as the setting.

A man reported the following dream:

> I am standing in front of a thick, high, stone wall which seems to snake on forever, kind of like the Great Wall of China. I know I have to get to the other side of the wall, but I can't find any way to go over, around, or through it.

The dreamer awoke, feeling hopeless and stuck. After some dream-work exploration, he prayed, "God, I'm really up against the wall. Please be with me here." A few moments later, the dreamer saw a soft light shining on part of the wall. It revealed a tiny hidden door just big enough for him to squeeze through by crawling on his belly. On the other side was a garden. His dreamwork continued as he explored the garden accompanied by the soft light that led him to the door.

10. *Finish your dream in God's presence.* Have you ever awakened before your dream was finished? Most people have. In an unfinished dream you never make it to shore, you don't find what was lost, you are still running from whatever was chasing you, or you barely miss the kiss of a really delicious person. Sometimes you can hit the snooze button and return to a particularly compelling dream for a few minutes, but often this is impossible.

Though disconcerting, an unfinished dream presents a wonderful opportunity for praying your dreams. Make some quick notes so you won't forget your dream. Then when you have time, ask God to shape your attention and your imagination and to be present with you. Enter into your dream again as if it were happening now, and let the dream roll on to a finish. In other words, let your imagination come up with an ending for your dream while you are awake.

You may imagine several endings. Again ask God to shape your awareness, to fade out the endings that are not truthful and bring forward the ending that is right for you. Invite the Holy One into your dream and its new ending and notice what happens. There will be a new twist to your plot and perhaps some new icons to work with. Pay particular attention to your body. The man who dreamed of the high stone wall discovered a new ending to his dream in this way.

Finishing a dream with God's help can take some time. Don't rush or force the process. I repeat: take time for silence, for waiting, for awareness to dawn slowly and spread through your body. Trust what is happening enough to record your prayerful dreamwork. Save thinking, evaluating, detecting patterns, or questioning for later. Be sure to thank God for gifting you with presence.

11. *As you continue to pray your dreams, at some point you will be aware of an invitation to change your life.* Praying your dreams is much more than a cozy chat, and God is much more than a loving witness to your growth, as important as that is. Invitations to change seem to happen a lot when you pray your dreams, so be warned! Think about it: is there any story of a genuine encounter with God in which someone was not invited to change in some way? As your prayer deepens, you may discover that you are being invited to:

- *Admit.* Admit that there are parts of yourself that you don't like and are not proud of. You might become aware of your jealousy and spitefulness, your fear of change, your addictions, your poses and facades, your helplessness to make changes on your own, your hanging on to the hoary past, or your walls that keep others out and isolate you. Also admit your gifts, if that is the particular challenge of your dream. You might recognize your flexibility, strength, or innate worth.

- *Surrender.* Surrender your fixed ideas about what it takes to make you happy, old habits of thought and behavior, ancient inflated or diminished ideas about yourself, your need to control the world, grudges you have nursed forever, or your insistence on shaping just how you will be healed.

- *Forgive.* Forgive your parents, your friends, your boss, the church, your ex, the opposite sex. Keep in mind that forgiveness is a process and does not happen overnight. Before you are finished, you will probably need to let yourself express your anger somehow in all its depth and poison, not necessarily in the presence of the one you are working to forgive. You may need some outside help with forgiveness, especially if you have been badly hurt.

- *Make room.* Make room for a new way to think about yourself, for God's forgiveness, for greater trust, for the impossibility of being perfect, for a new task, for cutting yourself some slack, for emotions that you have disowned, for a newly emerging part of yourself.

- *Ask for help.* When God invites you to change, God also helps you make the change. But don't expect big changes to be automatic or easy. Human growth, whether rapid or slow, is a process that involves commitment, hard work, mistakes, and side trips. Almost always you must grow into a change, even after you have stopped a certain behavior. You will need to make adjustments and ask for more help, always paying attention and surrendering as you go.

- *Explore the richness of other kinds of prayer.* Prayerful dreamwork is usually about your own healing and growth. But other kinds of prayer don't focus on you; the focus is on others or on God. Try praying for others (intercession) using faith imagination. Find ways to give thanks. Sing or dance or paint your praise. Find a congregation whose style attracts you and experiment with collective worship. Try praying some traditional prayers of the church with other people, even if you can't agree with every word. Try just sitting with the Holy One without asking for anything, and let God shape your encounter.

12. *Evaluate your dreamwork.* When you pray your dreams, can you be mistaken in what you perceive? Of course. Can your faith

imagination be inaccurate? Most certainly. Can you fool yourself by spinning a pretty tale? Oh yes. Dreamwork, with or without prayer, can be distorted. Your wishes, previous experiences, fear, distorted theology, emotional wounds, chemical imbalance, or a dozen other things can skew these processes. Being open to God is sometimes a tricky business, and evaluating your dreamwork and faith imagination experience a few days later, sometimes with another person, is crucial. A wise spiritual companion, a dreamwork partner, or a dreamwork group can be a great help in this regard. So can your record of dreamwork over time.

> **❝ Finishing a dream with God's help can take some time. Don't rush or force the process. ❞**

It is remarkable, however, how often prayerful dreamwork enables good emotional and spiritual growth. People are changed, sometimes in astonishing ways. They are set free to love more surely, live more joyously, pray more faithfully. They gain courage and wisdom. Sometimes suffering is not healed in the usual sense but made bearable through finding its meaning. Throughout this book are healing stories of dreamwork and faith imagination prayer. Furthermore, I am struck by just how often what comes forth in prayerful dreamwork and faith imagination is actually contrary to the expectations, mood, or theology of the dreamer and outside his or her conscious emotional and spiritual repertoire. Often there is a strong element of surprise, of discovery. The dreamer agrees with the man who dreamed of the chocolate-covered umbrella: "I could never have thought this up myself." So, despite the possibility of distortion, God seems to delight in healing and growing us through dreams.

A way to help you decide if you heard God's communication accurately is to look at the results of your prayerful dreamwork. If you can answer yes to the following questions, you are probably on the right track.

- Does my dreamwork reveal a God who loves me and is actively working to make me more whole?

- Does my dreamwork reveal the balanced truth about me, including my faults and need for healing, as well as my gifts?

- Does my dreamwork challenge and enable me to change for the better?

- Does my dreamwork help me be more loving, forgiving, and accepting of myself and others?

- Does my dreamwork leave some questions unanswered and some issues still in process?

- Does my dreamwork surprise me? Does the plot take on a different meaning than I had supposed?

But if you answer yes to any of the questions on the next page, consider getting professional help with someone well versed in dreamwork. Please understand, these questions are not a checklist to find out if you are crazy or sick! They are a way for you to decide if it makes sense to ask a knowledgeable and experienced person to support you as you strive to grow. Perhaps your particular journey is more difficult because of something that happened to you. Maybe you have been trying to bloom with a rock on your head. Sometimes help from someone who has explored his or her own depths can make all the difference. If the person you choose does not want to include prayer in your sessions, you still can use the suggestions in this book to pray your dreams.

- Does my dreamwork consistently leave me feeling condemned and blamed or somehow feeling worse?

- Do my dreams frequently have doomsday scenarios? (Read about nightmares in chapter 10.)

- Is my dreamwork almost solely sweet and rosy?

- Am I usually confused after working with my dreams?

- Do I sense that I am not going deep enough to benefit from my dreamwork?

- Do I lack the energy or hope to work on growing by myself?

- Do my dreams almost always terrify me?

## A FINAL WORD

While I was writing this chapter, I heard part of Psalm 139 read in church. For the first time it struck me that whoever first wrote down this beautiful psalm might have known a thing or two about finding God in dreams. Is it possible that the writer was referring to a series of dreams, or maybe a faith imagination reverie in which various scenes appeared in succession? Could the rough draft of this psalm have been noted in an ancient dream journal? You decide, but pay special attention to verse 18*b*.

> Where can I go from your spirit?
>     Or where can I flee from your presence?
> If I ascend to heaven, you are there;
>     if I make my bed in Sheol, you are there.
> If I take the wings of the morning
>     and settle at the farthest limits of the sea,

even there your hand shall lead me,
    and your right hand shall hold me fast.
If I say, "Surely the darkness shall cover me,
    and the light around me become night,"
even the darkness is not dark to you;
    the night is as bright as the day,
for darkness is as light to you.

          —Psalm 139:7-12

Then after a few verses extolling the all-knowing presence of God before he was born, and how "in secret" he was "intricately woven" "in the depths of the earth," and how God "knit [him] together" when he was an embryo, an "unformed substance," the psalmist writes,

I awake—I am still with you.
        —verse 18*b*, alternate reading

# CHAPTER TEN

# NIGHTMARES

**THE EXECUTIONER, THE FALLING TEETH, AND THE LANDING PLACE**

You wake up tense, your heart pounding, your body sweating, a scream rising in your throat. With great relief you realize that you have been dreaming. You turn on the light to help you wake up and chase away your nightmare. Even then your anxiety persists, for you begin to wonder if your nightmare signals that something really is wrong. Maybe your nightmare is a prediction that you are in danger, or a movie of a terrible and long forgotten event that actually happened, or an omen that someone you love is going to die. Maybe you're going crazy or coming down with a horrible illness.

In the middle of the night, such fears can feel close and real. Everyone knows dreamland is not always a beautiful place. Nightmares can terrify, disrupt sleep, and disturb your waking equilibrium. Most of us would be delighted if we never had another nightmare.

As awful as "bad dreams" feel, however, when you explore them, they usually reveal your inner push toward health and integration. Most nightmares are like any other dreams except that they produce the unpleasant emotions of fear or revulsion.

Remember, nearly every part of a dream points to some part of you, so in a nightmare look for an icon of some part of yourself that scares you silly. Expect to discover that those disowned and greatly feared parts of you are actually bringing gifts, although sometimes in a dreadful wrapping. You may have already guessed that exploring nightmares is not for wimps!

"Remember, nearly every part of a dream points to some part of you, so in a nightmare look for an icon of some part of yourself that scares you silly."

In nightmares you can be pursued by a monster that actually turns out to be your strength, your desire for change, your healthy anger, or your vigorous sexuality. You can experience death, the death of something no longer needed in you. You can kill, that is, get rid of, a false belief about yourself that holds you back. You can also stop killing off some good part of yourself, once your nightmare allows you see what you are doing. You can unchain a part of yourself that you have kept locked up. You can confront a nasty icon that is standing in for a nasty part of you. You can meet and learn to nourish your inner child, who may be suffering greatly. You can face the truth that you are capable of violence and love, stupidity and wisdom, fear and courage. Remember, the truth can set you free, but at first it can scare you out of your wits!

You can approach the vast majority of nightmares as you would any other dream. In fact, the vivid images of nightmares make them particularly good candidates for dreamwork. When you have a nightmare, face it as best you can. Record it in some way. Greet it as a gift. Thank God for it. Be curious about discovering its message. Play and pray the various icons, and let them have conversations with each other. Keep especially alert for God icons in the symbols of your nightmare. If you haven't discovered God already in your nightmare, invite God into the plot and see what happens.

However, work with nightmares is not always that easy. Your fear itself could distort the healing message or even keep you from exploring your nightmare altogether. In fact your dream may be reflecting what Fritz Perls calls your "catastrophic expectation." A catastrophic expectation is a fear of the terrible upheaval that will surely occur if you venture outside your carefully guarded inner boundaries. The sanest part of you knows these fears are baseless and irrational, but to your clutching stomach and tense muscles, your catastrophic fear feels absolutely genuine. Here are some examples of catastrophic expectations:

- If I really express my anger, I'll tear everything apart. I'll explode and destroy everything. No one and nothing will be left. Or else I'll go crazy or have a heart attack.

- If I start crying, I'll never stop.

- Who will I be if I quit being helpless?

- If I give up being responsible for everything, everything will fall apart.

- If I'm not useful, I have no value as a person.

Nightmares about nuclear bombs and other disasters are often metaphors of a greatly feared inner change about to erupt. If you are the kind of person who carries a tightly sealed capsule of old fear, tears, and anger, you may be especially prone to disaster dreams. Remember, your being is always pushing for health. Something in you wants to process old feelings so you can live your life in freedom and joy.

Change is always in the cards. So if part of you pushes for change and another part of you struggles to keep yourself under control, tension and fear result. Your nightmare does you a big favor by getting your attention and painting a dramatic picture of what is going on inside of you.

> **"When you have a nightmare, face it as best you can. Record it in some way. Greet it as a gift. Thank God for it. Be curious about discovering its message."**

If you are too frightened to face your nightmare, here are some things to try:

- Find a companion/witness who is not afraid of your nightmare. This might involve working with a mature friend, a therapist, or a pastoral counselor.

- Resolve to work with your nightmare as if you believe it has something positive to offer. Your own experience is a good teacher. The more you discover gifts in your own nightmares, the less afraid you become.

- Tell God how afraid you are, and ask to be shown how to gently ease into your nightmare. Then pay attention to any hunches you might have about which dream icon to focus on first.

- Ask God to enter your nightmare scenario with you. Open your imagination to experience for yourself how God is redeeming your worst nightmare.

- Read the following stories of terrifying nightmares that revealed messages of healing and transformation to the dreamers. Sometimes just knowing some examples of positive nightmares can reduce your fear of your own.

## THREE HEALING NIGHTMARES

### THE EXECUTIONER

Years ago a woman with a new PhD had a horrific nightmare in which she was expected to be an executioner. Back then her field of expertise bore a big stamp that said, "MEN ONLY!" Her very presence threatened her male colleagues, and she experienced daily hostility from them.

> I am in the execution chamber of a prison where there is a man strapped into an electric chair. I have the assignment of throwing the switch that will send thousands of volts into his body. I am full of revulsion and horror. This is awful! I don't want to kill him, but I know I must.
>
> As I stand in front of him, I see that his eyes are soft and his lips are trembling. He is helpless and frozen like a rabbit caught in headlights just before it is hit. I feel pity for him, but I know I will be the one to die if I don't carry out my assignment. I am terrified, trapped, nauseous, but I slowly reach for the switch. Just before I touch it, I wake up panicky and disoriented.

Later that same day, the shaken dreamer decided to play the executioner and the prisoner and let them have a conversation. There were many elements of the dream that she did not address: the prison, the switch, the electric chair, the nameless giver of the terrible assignment. Even so, working on just two icons of her dream began an important interior shift for her.

EXECUTIONER: I hate this! I don't want to fry you. I'm not a killer, for pete's sake! This is horrible! But they say I have to throw the switch.

PRISONER: I am strapped down and helpless and scared. I am about to die, but I am not a bad person. You have power over me and think you have to kill me, but I know you don't want to. You don't really have to kill me.

EXECUTIONER: But it's my assignment. If I don't kill you, I'll die myself. I have to be strong. . . . I *always* have to be strong!

PRISONER: Look at me. You see my soft eyes, my trembling lips. My crime is that I am vulnerable and afraid, and you can't stand it. You can't stand my vulnerability, so you threw me in jail and then strapped me down. You have me all trussed up and out of sight. You are so afraid of me . . . so afraid of my vulnerability you almost killed me off. . . . Aha! You are so afraid of *your* vulnerability that you have the impulse to kill me off, the soft, vulnerable part of yourself. Well, don't do it. You think being strong is everything, but without me you can't really do anything. You can't be a whole person.

EXECUTIONER: Oh, God! . . . I almost hear you saying, "Apart from me you can do nothing" [John 15:5]. . . . I need to undo the straps and let you out. That would be so much better than killing you. But if I let you out, I'll get slaughtered out there. There are a lot of people who would like for me to get weak and disappear so they won't have to deal with me anymore.

PRISONER: You need me, and you know it. The truth is, without me you will become a cold, unfeeling bitch.

EXECUTIONER: Damn, this is scary! (Her face crumples as she pantomimes undoing the straps and then, weeping, hugs the prisoner.) I'm going to need some time to assimilate this. I don't know anymore how to be vulnerable and soft, but I guess I'm willing for you to teach me. I'm still afraid of being afraid. . . . God help me.

Her dreamwork concluded with a prayer for courage and that she would learn to claim, and maybe even celebrate, her softness and vulnerability. She asked that she be enabled to integrate this newly rescued inner prisoner with her strength and ability to stand up for herself.

Those accustomed to dream analysis might point out that dreaming of a man in an electric chair with the dreamer in control of his fate surely points to rage at men. The hostility of her male colleagues supports this interpretation. It all makes sense. The trouble is, her own exploration took her in a different direction that was no less scary but more surprising and, I believe, more accurate for her at the time. She made a life-changing discovery while working on the execution dream.

I also believe that if she had worked on the dream a second time, she might in fact have encountered her anger at men. Furthermore, this new spin on her dream would not negate her former work but would add to it in some way. Remember, GPC dreamwork does not focus on analysis but on the discovery of and cooperation with an ongoing interior *process* of healing. We can be confident that if rage were inside her, it would surface again. As a matter of fact, she did contact her rage at a future time—when she was ready to face it.

## THE FALLING TEETH

A few months later the same young woman had another nightmare, this one not nearly as scary. The dream plot itself gives evidence of much inner growth.

> My teeth are falling out, fast. The roots are getting soft, and then my teeth are just falling out of my mouth. I'm getting soft, and my teeth are falling out, one by one. What will I do without my teeth? I want to glue them in somehow. I'm afraid more parts of me will fall away. I feel scared and out of control, and I wake up.

Here is what happened when the dreamer worked on this new dream:

DREAMER: I need you, teeth! Don't go away! Something is really wrong! How can you just fall out all at once? I feel so helpless to stop you.

TEETH: You really don't need us anymore. We are dying. It's okay. It's time for us to die. We are an old part of you that is falling away. You don't need to stop us; in fact you can't. You are helpless and getting soft in your roots, just like the man in the execution dream. Only now you are not as scared. And you really don't need such big ferocious teeth! You don't need to have such a bite! It's okay to let down your strong wall a little more.

DREAMER: But how can I defend myself?

TEETH: Your strength is not dying. You still have it and will be able to use it when you want. Having to be strong and tough all the time is what's dying. You're learning to ask for help and to let people see your weakness. You're finding a way to have both softness and strength.

The woman had been shifting between two pillows representing herself and her falling teeth. Now she sat between the two pillows. Touching both pillows, she said, "Gosh, I can really feel my strength and softness coming together. . . . It's like I know I have backbone, but my spine is supple and soft. This is great. *I* feel great! I feel more whole, and kind of new."

I have known this woman for many years and can vouch that the two nightmares, "The Executioner" and "The Falling Teeth," triggered a profound transformation that has now lasted half a lifetime.

THE LANDING PLACE

A recurring nightmare plagued a dreamer for years. In his dream he is always falling, falling, hurtling, plummeting, tumbling through limitless space, terrified and shrieking. Although he always wakes up before impact, he cannot shake the fear that one day he won't wake up in time and will die in his sleep. Each time he has the falling nightmare, he stays awake for hours afterward with all the lights on, drinking warm milk, willing his thudding heart and surging adrenaline to calm down.

The man came to an Opening to Grace workshop to explore this troubling dream. Remembering that the missing element in a dream is usually important, I asked, "Be your landing place, would you? Be the place where you would land if you didn't wake yourself up. Talk to the one who is falling through space."

He trembled, certain that the landing place had been lurking down there for years, sucking him downward, waiting for the opportunity to mangle his body. Nevertheless, after a prayer for courage he was intrigued enough to give it a go. He closed his eyes, breathed deeply, and went inside himself to search for the words that wanted to be spoken. With a hesitant voice punctuated by long silences he said,

> I am your landing place. . . . You have been falling toward me for years, . . . but you've never let yourself land. . . . I know you are scared to death, but . . . I am not here to destroy you. . . . I love you. . . . I will catch you and protect you. . . . Fall into my arms, dear one.

He stared upward, wide-eyed and slack-jawed. Expecting a death-watch over his gory corpse, he got a surprise party instead, complete with welcoming host, good friends, blazing birthday cake, jazz band, and confetti. At that moment his fear vanished.

As the retreat group gathered around him to touch and pray, he was already crying tears of joy and release. He said, "Yes, yes, yes, I am ready to fall into your arms. Help me land. Thank you, thank you, thank you for waiting, for being there." Shiny after our prayers, breathing out all the terror in the world, and feeling goofy with relief, he said, "Moon to Houston. The *Eagle* has landed. It was a long flight, but I think the nightmare is over." Then he laughed and laughed, pulling the whole retreat group into his belly guffaws.

Years have proved him right. The falling dream never recurred, and he is still learning what it means to live joyfully in "the arms of God."

## HOUSES THAT ARE ALIVE

Brian, a student in a GPC training group, came to a session on dreamwork saying,

> I never dream. When I was a child I had a terror dream that came back night after night. I would run into my parents' bedroom screaming, still seeing the dream in vivid detail, even though I knew I was awake and could hear my parents trying to calm me down. It's not surprising I had trouble sleeping as a kid, and I still do now.

> I was in kid therapy for a while, but it didn't do any good. No one was able to identify any big childhood stress. My parents were loving, and nothing bad happened to our family. Honestly, I had a pretty good childhood, except for my horrible nightmares.

> Even now, I'm still afraid I'll have that same nightmare. I'm not sure how, but I found a way to block out my dreams. I just don't want to go there. So, I couldn't have a dream for this class. I'm not sure I even want to get into anyone else's dreams. I may just watch today.

The class assured Brian it was fine if he chose to observe for now, and he sat back, looking relieved. He was well aware that in our class no one would push him to do anything he was not ready to do.

A few hours later, Brian decided to join in as the class worked with an imaginary dream. As he imaginatively enters the fake dream, he is riding in a car. Abruptly Brian veers away from the made-up dream and encounters a stranger who tells him, "Get out of the car. I'm going to stay with you. Come with me." Brian willingly follows, and soon he finds himself on a high footbridge in a park, where the stranger invites him to rest. He is a little afraid to stay there; the footbridge is high and a little rickety, but something about the stranger invites trust, so Brian lies down on the bridge. (He physically lies on the carpet.) Within one minute he is gasping and weeping, for his childhood nightmare is back in all its terrifying power.

> Oh no, the buildings! The buildings are back again! The big buildings all have mouths and eyes, and they can move. There are moving up and down and are coming toward me. They are after me! They will eat me up! Oh, no no no no!

By this time Brian is huddled on the floor, whimpering like a small child. I ask if he is willing to stay with his inner process, or if he would prefer to shut it down for now. Brian tells us he is willing to go on. Almost immediately he adds wonderingly,

> You know, these buildings sort of look like cartoons. In all that therapy I never told anyone the buildings look like cartoon figures. Even as a kid I sorta knew—and didn't know—they were cartoons, but by then the nightmare had a life of its own. The nightmare would always end with the buildings chasing me, and I would run screaming into my parents' bed.

I asked him if he had ever gone into one of the buildings. No, he said, but since the stranger invited him to be in his dream again, he was willing. With the stranger accompanying him, he enters a building and discovers to his stunned astonishment that the inside of the building is a church.

> I'm in a church with the stranger, and suddenly I'm not afraid anymore. Somehow everything's okay. Everything's okay! Oh God, everything is okay. I can't believe it . . . but everything's okay.

Brian paused a minute to breathe in those surprising words, "Everything's okay, everything's okay!" Then he continued,

> Now I'm back on my parents' bed. I'm a boy and a man at the same time. I see the scary houses floating in the air, but now the one in the middle is

a church with steeple and cross. The church is attached to a string that just materialized. My six-year-old son is on the bed with me and reaches back toward the foot of the bed for the string, and suddenly the church is inside a balloon. Smiling, he hands me the balloon, and the other scary houses just fade away. With that smile I have a sense that all the buildings turned into churches, and I know that somehow my nightmare has been redeemed.

Brian sat up on the floor, his eyes still wet, still a little stunned. None of us knew just how the dream was "redeemed," nor did we ever find out what the dream meant. We were content not to know. In thanksgiving we prayed for him, asking that he would be able to live into this healing.

Toward the end of the class, Brian, a minister with much experience dealing with troubled churches, mused:

> Could I as a child have had the foreknowledge that dysfunctional churches can devour ministers? And that they have "eyes" and "mouths" that can make a pastor's life a living hell? Or maybe God used the transformed dream to heal my present life. And how in the world did working on a fake dream lead to the deepest work of my life? . . . I guess it's a mystery I'm content to live with. All I know is that what had been so terrifying is now a gentle gift.

Four months later I called him to ask how his dreamwork had settled. "I've been feeling very grounded since the dreamwork," he said. "When I think of the nightmare now, I no longer gasp in fear. Instead I see Christ, the 'stranger' in my dream, leading me into a church, and my son carrying the balloon. Although I still don't understand it, I feel the redemption all over again. I notice that I am less upset with church squabbles and struggles because I'm more accepting of the church folk for who they are. And there has been a huge change in my spiritual life. I feel more trusting, more led by God. I also have a new commitment to diet and exercise, and I definitely have more energy. That dreamwork triggered a very peaceful resolution."

## EXCEPTIONS

You may have noticed that I was careful to write that *most* nightmares can be approached like any other dream. Some rare types of nightmares have different origins from ordinary dreams, and thus they don't fit the usual pattern.

*First, if you suddenly have a lot of nightmares, check to see whether nightmares are a possible side effect of a medication you are taking.* Sometimes nightmares are the result of your brain on a drug, rather than a glimpse of truth about yourself. If a drug could be causing your nightmares, ask your doctor whether you might try another medication. If that is not possible, at least you can console yourself with the idea that those drug-induced nightmares are not intrinsic to you.

*Second, if you have experienced a traumatic event that you have not fully processed, you might dream a fairly realistic replay of the event.* (In my experience, dreams replay events that are already in conscious memory.) Replay nightmares can be triggered by such experiences as childhood sexual abuse, rape, natural disasters, war, and accidents. (Many New Yorkers had 9/11 dreams after that day of terror.) Replay nightmares are awful because you keep reexperiencing your trauma, sometimes for years. After a while you may be afraid to go to sleep, and your inevitable fatigue compounds your anxiety.

If you think you are having trauma replay nightmares, try to see them as a sign that your dreams are inviting you to work toward healing. I know from experience that with hard work and prayer, traumas are usually healable, but trauma work is not easy to do by yourself. You will probably need professional help. Ask around; get recommendations. Try to find someone who is compassionate and experienced with both trauma and dreamwork. Choose someone who will let you work at your own pace. In this context your replay nightmare can provide special help in your healing because it is a good setting for faith imagination prayer. Try praying your nightmare as described in the last chapter. You may be surprised at what happens when you invite God into your trauma nightmare.

*Third, a few nightmares reveal the presence of evil.* In over thirty years of working with dreams and trauma, I remember only a few instances of genuine evil in a dream. I didn't want to admit it at first, but finally I had to conclude that very occasionally evil puts in an appearance in a dream. Please pay special attention to what I'm about to say. *In my experience, dreams of evil are extremely rare. You can't just go by your feelings here; most of what feels evil in dreams turns out to be a part of yourself that you are afraid of, or some toxic belief about yourself that you swallowed a long time ago.* Do all you can to investigate your dream in the ordinary way first. Pray a lot with a mature and balanced person. Conclude that evil is present only as a last resort.

> **❝** Most of what feels evil in dreams turns out to be a part of yourself that you are afraid of, or some toxic belief about yourself that you swallowed a long time ago. **❞**

To be honest, I debated about whether to mention evil at all, because I was afraid some of you readers might jump to the conclusion that evil is responsible for all that is wrong in your life. Or you may feel that even the most incidental reference to evil sounds just plain nutty. Even worse, I feared that you would label an unintegrated part of yourself as evil, leading you to further reject something in you that actually holds great gifts.

Deciding that your dream contains an icon of evil should be a careful process in which you and at least one other person finally conclude that the suspected icon holds absolutely no gifts or goodwill. Instead, the icon brings a message that is set on destroying all that is good and healthy in you. Because of the strong possibility of your denial, discernment of evil is best done with someone who has long experience with dreamwork, is not afraid to entertain the idea of evil, is mature and balanced, and has some idea of how to proceed if evil is indeed present.

If genuine evil is fueling your nightmare, your dreamwork will not be about integration but eradication. Detailed instruction in this regard is beyond the scope of this book, but here are the main things to remember:

- Don't jump to quick conclusions.

- Don't get fascinated with evil.

- Don't scare yourself.

- Don't mistake your fear of yourself for evil.

- Remind yourself that God is in charge.

- Focus on God's power instead of on evil. It's really quite simple to order evil away in the name of Christ.

Below I tell the story of one dream that presented an icon of evil, and how the dreamer and I responded. This short account is not a how-to manual but a story that I hope will allay your anxiety.

## THE THUGS

Beverley came to her weekly session with a disturbing dream. In the dream she comes downstairs in her house to find a group of nasty-looking thugs in her living room. "Who are you, and what are you doing in my house?" she demands. "Lucifer!" they snarl. "And we are here to destroy you. You can't stop us. It's just a matter of time before we kill you." Beverley wakes up terrified.

Although the thugs certainly sounded scary, Beverley and I discerned carefully over a period of several weeks, praying the question of whether we should order the thugs away. Both of us wanted to be certain that the thugs were not simply an unintegrated part of Beverley. Gestalt dreamwork revealed that the thugs were completely bent on destroying Beverley's faith and wrecking her relationship with a man she loved; we both received confirmation of this separately as we prayed. I also had the clear sense that despite their threats, ordering the dream thugs away would not be difficult.

With minimal fuss and in the context of a regular session, Beverley and I demanded in the name of Jesus that the thugs leave her. Beverley exhaled deeply a few times, immediately the thugs obeyed, and Beverley and I both knew it. The result in Beverley was not really dramatic; she just had the feeling of more space inside her body.

By the next week she was sure that she was more able to experience her feelings. Before, her emotions had been wispy, muted, and often inaccessible. After, she was feeling joy, tears, passion, and anger with surprising intensity. Her faith was greatly strengthened, and she felt that she had come alive in a new way. Her man friend loved the changes in her, and their relationship deepened.

## FORETELLING DREAMS

Foretelling dreams—instances in which you dream of something that actually happens later—are not always nightmares. Stories of foretelling dreams abound and can render dreamers unable to completely dismiss their fear that their nightmare is actually a glimpse of a terrible future. In my experience, *dreams almost never reveal direct foreknowledge.* I am quite sure that some dreamers assume they have seen the future in a dream, when actually they have experienced a coincidence.

However, I cannot deny that genuine foretelling dreams do exist, although I believe them to be quite unusual. A favorite story in my family is how my mother dreamed of meeting my father. In her dream she meets a fellow student on the University of Michigan library steps. He falls and drops his books; she helps him up. He asks her to play tennis; she says yes. The next morning her dream scenario played out in real life exactly as she dreamed it. What really captured her heart that day was beating him easily at tennis and discovering that he was still interested in her. A year later she married "the man of my dreams." Her foretelling dream served their marriage well; Mom and Dad had an easy relationship of genuine equality and friendship. They were still comfortably and deeply in love when they died in a plane crash in their late forties.

I love this story of my mother's dream, but frankly I am not sure how to understand it. Foretelling dreams certainly don't fit neatly into Gestalt theory, and I haven't had much experience with them in any case. Occasionally I have heard someone I know describe a foretelling dream, and the Bible records some stunners. All I can say is that such dreams point to a realm of time-bending mystery that we cannot control or even understand.

Foretelling dreams do not erode my belief that all dreams are a gift of God that can bring healing, both personal and social. Respected biblical scholar Walter Brueggemann writes of the foretelling dreams of four biblical movers and shakers: Jacob, Pharaoh, Nebuchadnezzar (with Daniel, his dream interpreter), and one of the magi. In an article titled "Holy Intrusion: The Power of Dreams in the Bible," he says, "In all four cases, the course of public history, with its determined configurations of power, is disrupted by a hidden truth [a dream] designed to create new possibilities."[1] You can read about the dreams in Genesis 28:10-22; Genesis 41:14-24; Daniel 4:19-37; and Matthew 2:12.

It's important to remember that biblical stories often distill years, even centuries, of wisdom into just a few verses. The Bible is not a dreamwork how-to book. We don't know the details of just how biblical people concluded that certain dreams were revelations from God. I believe, though, that they regarded dreams as a holy venue for God to be revealed. "Big" biblical dream stories are surely the result of someone approaching a dream prayerfully with an open heart to discern what God might be communicating to the dreamer, acting on this discernment, and paying attention to the result.

---

1. *The Christian Century* 122, no. 13 (June 28, 2005), 28–31.

# CHAPTER ELEVEN

# BIG DREAMS

## COOL, CLEAR WATER

Occasionally a dream appears that marks or facilitates a major turning point in a life, or gives meaning to life-changing events. Sometimes called "big dreams," these highly significant, emotionally rich dreams are both rudders and beacons, and have great staying power.[1] They can be catalysts that change the course of a life. Wise dreamers return to them again and again over the years, not only to remind themselves of the original dreamwork but also to mine these important dreams for new directions. Dreamers hit the jackpot when they have big dreams; they are literally the gifts of a lifetime. Examples of big dreams are "The Holy Duck" (p. 91), "The Executioner" (p. 123), and "The Talking Cat" (p. 93).

Richard, pastor of a rural church in the American Midwest, is from Australia, where his ex-wife and adult children still live. "Cool, Clear Water" first appeared in Richard's life about six years ago as a disturbing, recurring nightmare. It was as if the dream itself was saying, "Hey, you—yeah, you! Pay close attention here!"

Richard's reaction to his big dream has gone through several stages, with the message of the dream changing as Richard has grown. Over the years, the dream took on an increasingly positive spin as a valued truth-teller, and his most recent dreamwork with "Cool, Clear Water" left him vibrating with joy. From my own experience with big dreams, I predict that Richard will be discovering the full impact of

"Cool, Clear Water" for a long time. It will be like yeast bubbling away quietly until the new bread rises once again. And again.

## COOL, CLEAR WATER

My wife, Harriett, and our two children, Jennifer and Charles, are with me in a beautiful sailboat. I am 28, Harriett is 26, Jennifer is 10, and Charles is 8. This doesn't make sense. We can't be these ages together, but here we are. I have always wanted to have such a lovely sailboat. And now we are on the sea, not too far out. The sun is shining, and the sail is full of air. I feel wonderful and so exhilarated.

We are sailing along nicely when a huge wave comes out of nowhere and slams into the boat. Our beautiful sailboat flips over, and we are all thrown into the sea. Suddenly everything is chaos. Jennifer is splashing toward me with big, wide eyes. I yell to my wife, Harriett, to save Charles while I save Jennifer. Harriett is thrashing about helplessly and screams back, "I can't swim!" She is keeping herself afloat but is making no effort to help. She doesn't seem to be a bit worried about the children. I see that it's my job to rescue everyone.

Suddenly the sea is no longer turbulent, and the small waves are reflecting the sun, but we are still in great danger. I am terribly afraid. I am trying to get to my children, who are desperately flailing in the water. Jennifer looks reproachful that I'm letting her down. Charles is terrified and doesn't know which parent to go to. I finally get hold of both kids and barely manage to hold them up, but I can't reach Harriett. I have to let her go.

The sadness, the sadness, the sadness . . . anger under the sadness . . . and guilt. . . . Harriett won't help. I can't save the kids. I failed them. We can't return to the boat; it's upside down and going under. We have to swim to shore, have to get on solid ground. Even though I'm a strong swimmer, I'm afraid I'm not strong enough to get both kids to shore.

The dream always ends with deciding which child to rescue. I wake up feeling terrible for taking them out in the boat and then not being able to rescue them both.

When Richard first dreamed "Cool, Clear Water," he knew that the dream plot flashed a remarkably clear image of the emotional currents surging around his divorce a few years earlier. Before the divorce he was "sailing along"; then the "huge wave" broke over the family and capsized their life together. Their "boat" could no longer be trusted as a refuge, and Harriett's nearly pathological helplessness and narcissism had indeed angered and saddened him. The kids were scared and bewildered, even though they were nearly adults when the divorce was finalized. Jennifer in particular felt betrayed. Richard felt enormous guilt for the whole mess, made worse by an inner mandate to somehow "rescue" the kids, making sure they didn't "go down" with the trauma of their parents' split.

> " Big dreams can be catalysts that change the course of a life. "

Richard's earliest work on this dream had to do with recognizing the emotional truths presented by his dream plot and with giving up, as best he could, his efforts to rescue his children. He saw that he was attempting an impossible task: to "get them to shore," that is, to shield them from any pain or distress. Of course he was unable to do this; no one could be "strong enough" to insure a painless life for someone else. He further recognized that Jennifer and Charles could indeed swim for themselves; they had resilience and resources and could process the divorce in their own ways. Even Harriett was actually a fine swimmer, for all her pretended helplessness. She too bore some of the responsibility for their capsized marriage. Clearly, it was not all Richard's fault. Recognizing intellectually the truth in his dream-work was quite helpful, and although Richard's guilt gradually began to recede, it did not completely go away.

Several lonely years passed. By then, Richard had become involved with a woman who was in love with him and eager to marry. Richard was not ready for another marriage and said so. The two broke up, got together again, and then broke up a second, third, and fourth time. Neither was quite able to leave the tumultuous relationship, which remained locked in a veritable tug-of-war. Her urgent "Yes, now!" equaled Richard's vehement "No, I can't!"

During this time, Richard worked on the dream again. An important part of this second round of dreamwork came when he spoke as his daughter Jennifer talking to the sea:

> JENNIFER: I'm paddling around in circles, not knowing where to go, getting exhausted. I'm just treading water. The more I try to stay afloat, the more I lose energy. I feel my energy draining away, just draining away. I can't keep this up much longer. I'm going under, and no one can rescue me. You, sea, are strong, and will overpower me. You are pulling me under, and I'm going to drown.

> THE SEA: Yes, you can't fight me. I am going to have you. You can fight all you want, but you are mine.

> JENNIFER: No, I'm not yours! You're trying to control every part of me, and I'm tired of it. You don't care how much I struggle against drowning. You don't listen to me when I say no. You are drowning me!

By then a new awareness ignited in Richard: the sea was an icon of the shame and exhaustion planted inside him by his demanding and perfectionist parents, and sharply revealed in relation to his woman friend. He indeed experienced her as one who demanded his acquiescence and shamed him when he said no, exhausting him and pulling him down. I invited Richard to ask the Holy One to join him in this struggle. Immediately Jesus appeared in Richard's mind's eye but seemingly did not react directly to the issue of his friendship. Instead, he told Richard, "I am with you in this. I will make sure your family is safe." Then Richard saw Jesus towing Jennifer, Charles, Harriett, and himself to the shore. What tremendous relief! They were all safe, rescued, warming up, celebrating the solid ground.

Soon, however, the kids and Harriett drifted away from the shore in separate directions, each knowing that they were not rescued to be together, but so they could live their own lives. Richard, left alone with Jesus, was grateful, saddened, and acutely aware of his aloneness. The image of standing on the beach all alone, his family scattered, stayed with Richard and made it really difficult to imagine making a clean break from his woman friend. Even though Jesus was "with him on the beach," he explained that he "still needed a real person to be a friend," even if that friendship was difficult. And even though he was making room for the idea that Jesus had rescued his family and that it wasn't his job anymore, his loneliness, shame, and mild depression continued.

Fast-forward to Richard in a GPC practicum about two years later. We were working with dreams that day, and during the opening prayer for the class, Richard's sailboat dream forcefully "came from nowhere" into his awareness. He had not thought about the dream for a while, but there it was, compelling his attention once more.

Another student served as Richard's guide for the dreamwork. Even as Richard told the dream this time, he experienced it differently. He was surprised to notice that when the family was dumped into the water, "the sea is not cold but cool and invigorating." His guide invited him to be the sea. He said,

> I am the sea. I'm not still but jumping up and down. There are depths in me that go down into darkness. I'm holding these people up, giving them

buoyancy. I make it possible for them to be alive—but their thrashing around muddies my water. There is deep darkness underneath me—lifeless darkness, no bubbles, no fish, no creatures, no shadows. I am full of dead darkness with no bottom. I am too deep to see into; light only shines a little way into me. People only know the top of me. There are depths to me that are not seen. They are unplumbed, even by me.

He paused to breathe and take in what he had just said. Everyone was silent, giving him space. He continued,

There is no harm down there, just unknown depths. As I sink further, I see that my darkness does not go on forever; there is only a layer of it. Underneath is beautiful clear water. I'm cold and refreshing, sparkling clean water, clear water. There is a lot of life in me.

His voice broke, and he stopped breathing as if he couldn't quite believe what he had just said. His guide reminded him to breathe in the life-affirming image of himself as cold, clear water sparkling with life, and to say the words again. And again. As he repeated those surprising words, he began to weep.

I can't see my darkness anymore. I'm peaceful, alive, alert. I have a life-giving refreshing depth to me that I never knew was there. I contain life! Refreshing beauty! Oh, such . . . joy!

Richard was now sobbing full-throated, releasing old patterns of thought, reactions, and behavior and making room for the new, almost as if he was being reconfigured inside. His classmates were praying silently, pulling for him.

RICHARD: That muddy strata shows how other people have muddied me up with their punishments and criticisms and judgments. I'm angry that they have stirred all that mud into me.

GUIDE: Can you tell that to the people who muddied you up?

RICHARD (speaking to these people): You have made me dirty, dead. You only know me as a muddy pool. You've got to see deeper. Down here I'm not shallow. I'm not a muddy mess. Not at all.

Richard is now gently cradling his stomach in his arms. When his guide asked him what his arms were doing, he replied,

I'm holding myself, loving myself, as clear, cold water. I feel so stimulating and refreshing! I have never felt this before, but I'm an enormous, bottomless pool of goodness!

Then, speaking to the ones who had muddied him up (who were not named in this dreamwork session), he said, "I wish I could let my mud settle so you can see me. I want you to swim and be refreshed in me." Richard paused, breathing deeply. "Actually this mud doesn't need to settle. It needs to be filtered out instead." Spontaneously he prayed, "Holy Spirit, please come and filter out my mud and murkiness so that people might be refreshed in relation to me. Please throw in your net and take care of my layer of mud." He paused, alert, open, breathing deeply, waiting. The rest of us in the room watched, praying silently. After a few minutes, Richard finally spoke.

I see Jesus throwing his net in and gathering up the mud by absorbing it with cotton wool. He is filtering out my murkiness. As he draws out the dirty cotton wool, clear water drips back in. Now people can see way down. People love diving in such clear water. I remember diving into deep, clear water in the Greek Islands and seeing all the way to the deep bottom. . . . I'm beautiful, clear, clean, refreshing. I give joy and delight, and I feel joy and delight.

He opened his eyes and looked at each of us, his glowing face wet with tears, his body relaxed and loose, his gaze full of love. "I haven't felt joyful like this for many years," he told us. "My joy is in my heart and chest, and it stretches to my toes, and then it circles back up to the top of my head. My head especially is translucent water right now."

The session ended with the group gathered around him to pray that Richard would be enabled to live into this wonderful transformation and that his new joy would permeate other areas of his life: memories, experiences, ideas, beliefs. Together we shared how moved we were to be witnesses to a marvelous and holy synergy that gave us a glimpse of a Richard we hadn't met before.

Seven months later I contacted Richard to ask permission to write his story and to find out how his dreamwork with the class had settled. "How has your dreamwork played out over the last few months?" I asked. "Did your joy fade, or did it last?" Richard was eager to talk; I have never heard him be so voluble and enthusiastic. His words tumbled out: "That dreamwork almost totally transformed my life," he began.

> I feel such joy every time I realize that I am a person with beautiful depths. I'm freed in so many ways to live more fully. I can give my opinion now, actually believing that I have something worthwhile to contribute. If I have something to say, I just put it out there, and if I am not heard, I say it again. I'm finding out that people actually value what I have to say, even during church meetings!

> I know that part of this change is that I no longer allow people to treat me with disrespect. My parishioners would routinely disparage and even ridicule what I had to say. So would [my woman friend]. It's fine if we disagree—that's really okay—but I don't accept that what I say has no value. That's nonsense. I have much stronger boundaries now, and I am learning not to let others muddy my water.

> The higher-ups in the church are always urging me to do more, do more, do more, even though I already work very long hours. They expect me to bring in crowds of new people, even though our town is declining rapidly in population, and my little group of elderly parishioners doesn't have the stamina or resources to sustain any new programs. They hint that I am failing the church for not producing the results they want. I refuse to feel guilty over this situation any longer.

I realize at last that for years I have been holding on to old guilt and shame. I lived with guilt and shame, and others played into my low opinion of myself. That's how I would allow my water to get muddy—I could so easily be manipulated through my inner shame. That's how my parents treated me, and that's how it was in my marriage. I was always to blame for everything—it was just the way they all dealt with me. Even now my adult kids blame me alone for the divorce and all that is wrong in their present lives, even though neither of them is actively working with their personal issues. I'm no longer willing to bear all the responsibility for everyone's problems. I now see the divorce as a breath from God to bring healing to all of us.

Finding my own depths has helped me see the depths in others. I can now look past crabby comments and criticisms from church members, and my own irritation with them. Instead I see beauty and loveliness in them. I know I am a better pastor now because I can love my people much more deeply. More and more I am able to touch and relate to their depths instead of what they present on the surface.

I'm even able to entertain the idea of marriage again. With all that muddy guilt and shame, I couldn't imagine a real relationship. I was sure that once again I would let someone down and cause her pain. Any marriage was certain to fail, and it would be completely my fault. Now I am imagining a relationship of real intimacy and trust. I don't know what's ahead on the marriage front, but I am cautiously open to exploring.

One of the biggest changes in my life has been spiritual. Growing up, I was always taught that *my* sins nailed Jesus to the cross. I lived with a sort of suspended sentence that I could never get out from under. Whenever I did anything wrong, even a small thing, in my mind I was a murderer. I was a sinner who had crucified my Lord. Fundamentally I was bad to my core.

Richard holds several degrees in theology, including a professional doctorate, and for years has recognized that as a child, he absorbed a skewed theology of redemption and atonement. He knew perfectly well that a finger-shaking, condemning, angry God is a distortion of the gospel, and he never would have preached or taught along those lines. Nevertheless, the old damaging tapes still had insidious power to shape his sense of himself and his relationship to God. After the momentous dreamwork with our class, his spiritual orientation changed fairly rapidly.

> Now I know in my soul that of course I am not a murderer if I do something wrong. I am not perfect by any means, but now when I acknowledge that I have not lived up to the gospel, or when I feel a little depressed or uncertain, Jesus simply throws in the net, and the cotton wool again absorbs my muddiness. I am left with sparkling water full of life and refreshing coolness and joy. I believe that God most certainly recognizes—but does not focus—on my mud. I have the feeling that God sees and loves all of me but takes special delight in my sparkling water. That's who I was created to be, and God wants to heal me so I can be that more and more. That's my new picture of redemption now. I almost want to cry with joy.

Then Richard's voice became slower, more hesitant, as he spoke of the newest, most tender, gift from this dream.

> Lately I sense that the clear sea in the dream is not only me but also an icon of God. When I look at my own depths, I sense that somehow my depths mingle with God. I'm almost afraid to say this . . . but when I look at my depths, I also look at the presence of God . . . God in *me* . . . God in me. I am so very grateful.

About a month later, as I was preparing the final draft of this book, Richard wrote to say that his big dream was still reverberating. He said,

> When a good friend of mind suddenly started dating another man and speaking about the joy of her new relationship, I felt a deep sense of loss and sadness. As I prayed, I suddenly knew what the layer of deadness in my dream was all about. My deadness was my sexuality. I had tried to deaden my sexuality in my relationships with women.

> Growing up, I felt shame for having sexual feelings. I was taught they were wrong. In my marriage I was humiliated over and over when I could not satisfy my wife. I despaired of ever being able to bring joy and delight to a woman in this area, so I turned my sexuality off as best I could. I formed

friendships with people for whom I thought a sexual relationship was unimportant. These relationships soon became stagnant or conflicted. I feared another marriage, as I thought it would bring humiliation and shame.

My dream helped me realize that my experiences of sexual humiliation and shame were just people "muddying my water." Once again I saw Jesus throw his cotton wool net and filter out the muddiness of sexual shame and humiliation. Crystal-clear water dripped back into the sea. Now, sparkling bubbles reflected light as fish darted around with playful joy. I knew that God was affirming my sexuality, blessing it and giving it joyful life. . . . I am gathering courage to date people who will honor that side of me.

I tell Richard's story in detail because it beautifully summarizes Gestalt Pastoral Dreamwork and particularly illustrates the gift of big dreams. Let Richard's dreamwork remind you once more that

- Dreamwork is not magic but enables a process of emotional growth and change that may take some time.

- Dream icons can point to multiple realities and can carry more than one meaning.

- Intellectual understanding of a dream's message seems to be less important to the dreamer's growth than the discoveries that come from encountering the dream experientially.

- The message of a dream, particularly a big dream, shifts and deepens as the dreamer grows. In other words, the dreamer can experience his or her dream differently over time.

- God uses dreams both to reveal truth about the dreamer's life, and to show Herself/Himself in a way that addresses the unique matrix of the dreamer's spiritual wounds and hunger.

## UPDATE ON "THE FORGOTTEN ATTIC"

I believe that "The Forgotten Attic," dreamed when I first began writing this book about a year ago, is a big dream. Although I'm still in the early stages of exploring it and expect to hear from it often in the next few years, "The Forgotten Attic" has already begun to change my life in some important ways.

> " My dreamwork challenges me to 'stay awake.' Yours will challenge you to do the same. "

I'm now playing the viola and violin imperfectly but with new gusto, as my musical "must-be-perfect paralysis" fades a little. I don't apologize as much for imprecise intonation or even wrong notes. After all, I'm a beginner! The calluses on my left-hand fingertips are returning, and I'm starting to grow a new violin hickey on my neck. Actually I'm playing better than I have in a long time. The unaccompanied Bach sonatas for violin and viola are my old—and new—friends.

I bought a bike and a snappy-looking helmet six months ago, and I'm enjoying zooming around the neighborhood when the weather is good. I'm also working with a personal trainer to learn how to tone up my rusty body. Conveniently, she lives directly across the street from me and has a small gym in her basement. There I am most certainly a beginner. To my surprise, for the first time in my life I don't dislike "gym class," especially since I get to pick the exercise music. Hint to gym owners: try Vivaldi!

On so many fronts I'm discovering how very much I don't know, and I like the feeling. Cultivating a beginner's attitude at this stage of my life is not only exhilarating but also honest. I have much more to learn about how much there is to learn!

Getting rid of the scruffy stuffed owl in the attic was another step in reframing my teen years. I have come to appreciate more deeply my owlish adolescence, including the pain of being different and lonely. Because I was such an outsider, I learned early on to think outside the box and to find ways to feel all right about myself without receiving constant approval or applause. Because I had very few friends, I didn't experience much peer pressure. As painful as it was to be a loner, I was able to learn to be myself without much interference. My teenage feelings of self-consciousness and unattractiveness followed me far too long into adulthood, but these days, with the owl in the trash, I find I am more content to have an older woman's face and body, and sometimes I actually like how I look.

I've had more dreams about funny buildings, most of them really decrepit on the outside but full of treasures inside. (Do you sense a polarity here? Or a theme?) One dream featured a sharecropper shack I remember well from my Alabama childhood, complete with rotting steps and mangy hound dogs panting under the sagging porch. Although the sparsely furnished two-room house was held up by unsteady piles of flat rocks and had neither running water nor electricity, in my dream the house has been repaired and is full of intricate wooden chests, vividly painted whirligigs, amazing sculptures, and simple, beautiful furniture made of natural wood, including a small bed and couch. There are woodworking tools lying about, along with a number of unfinished projects. While still asleep I recognize that I am an unfinished project, and I have a sense of Jesus the carpenter sneaking around a corner where I don't quite see him.

Since dreaming "The Forgotten Attic," I have continued to be drawn in by the gorgeous, fascinating, "trinitarian" chest. Surely, I thought, I would discover that this special chest is an icon of God's presence. One day, with great expectation, I let the chest speak.

> THE CHEST: I am a beautiful chest, seamlessly made with three parts. My parts fit together so that I look whole. I am old and very valuable. Someone took a great deal of trouble over me when I was created. I am unique and rare. There is no one else like me anywhere.
>
> Even so, most people don't notice me. They go past me, intent on getting where they are going. To them I seem like just something old that's been around a long time. That's really okay with me. I know what I am, so I don't need them to see me. In fact, I don't want them to see me. If they did, some people might want a piece of me, and I would have no peace.
>
> Tilda, you must open my doors and drawers. I am beautiful on the inside too. And I contain secrets and gifts that you know nothing about.

Nice words, truth-filled words, but surely they did not point to the God who thundered to Moses, "I AM WHO I AM" (Exodus 3:14). Instead I recognized a part of myself that I already knew pretty well. Even so, my hunch persisted that the chest might be a God icon. Feeling that I just needed to go deeper, I decided to play the chest again. But here is where things got interesting. Instead of speaking as the chest, what came out of my mouth was a startling message resonating with God's love and, yes, thunder.

> Tilda, there is a part of you that constructed this chest to keep me in closed drawers. You didn't even know you were doing it. I won't be confined! Yes, the chest is beautiful, like a beautiful altar, but it is not me. I can't be kept in a chest or even on an altar. I am bigger than your idol of a pretty chest. Come away from the dusty attic that is you, for I am bigger than your psychology, your feelings, or your parts. Come and sit with me.

Whew! Still reflecting on that message weeks later, in the middle of a bout of writer's block, I found myself idly typing words for the space, the "no-thingness" in the attic. Again I recognized God speaking to my soul.

> SPACE: I am the space all around you. I am the air you breathe. I animate you. There is no place I am not. I hold everything about your life—treasures and gifts, as well as your junk and detritus and everything else you need to surrender. You can find hints of me in everything in the attic, even everything in the world. Look around and see me in everything, but know I am bigger than anything you see. I am both knowable and unknowable. Every time you breathe, remember I am here. I am surrounding you and preserving your life. And I have some surprises for you. Stay awake!
>
> ME (gulping): Uh, okay.

So much for my hunch about just how God would be revealed!

Still ahead is exploring the drawers of the chest. I sense that the drawers are important, so I have saved that piece for a retreat when I will have time to absorb whatever happens. I also have recorded other recent dreams that I want to play and pray:

- My father, who has been dead since I was sixteen, is dressed in his baggy tweed egghead suit, accessorized as usual with his pocket slide rule. He comforts me as I lean on his chest. I'm crying for all the suffering in the world.

- I am taking a train through a deep forest. The train stops in a clearing, and I get off. I find myself in a sunny meadow where I discover huge shiny green dinosaurs slowly moving their beautiful gossamer wings.

- I discover a fluffy white baby camel romping around my living room.

- I find a large, weeping sore on my leg.

- I am holding an old woman who has collapsed in a store. She dies peacefully in my arms as I pray for her.

So, my growth is a process full of surprises and turns, just as yours will be. My dreamwork challenges me to "stay awake." Yours will challenge you to do the same. I urge you to go for it. I believe your dreams are fabulous gifts, most certainly worthy of the time and attention it takes to unwrap them. And who knows? In one of your dreams you just might be surprised to find that the Holy One is filling your hunger, and maybe even mending your heart.

----

1. For a good introduction to current research on big dreams, see Rebecca Cathcart, "Winding Through 'Big Dreams' Are the Threads of Our Lives," *New York Times* (July 3, 2007), sec. D, 1– 2.

# DELIBERATELY
## SHUTTING *the* DOOR

Dreamwork can stir up emotions, sometimes at inconvenient moments. You may suddenly find yourself too tired, too rushed, or too afraid to welcome the emotional surprises that can accompany dreamwork. The following suggestions are most certainly not about denying that your emotions are present, or tensing up to control them, but deliberately shutting them down temporarily. Knowing how to shut down may give you a feeling of control, and opening up later on may seem less frightening. As I have already made clear, I recommend getting some professional help if you are terribly scared of what surfaces for you as you work with your dreams.

Here are two suggestions for how to temporarily shut the door on your dreams, one from the wisdom of Gestalt, and the other from the wisdom of prayer:

1. *Pay close attention to your five senses in the present moment.*

The idea here is that as long as you stay in the present moment, you are not awash in the past or worried about the future. As you do this exercise, don't name anything that was happening even one minute ago, or what you could expect one minute from now. Stay precisely in the present moment.

- *Look around and name aloud what you see.* Describe your surroundings in detail, for example: I see my bluish computer screen and a silver phone with lighted numbers behind clear plastic. Both are sitting on a brown wooden desk. I see a greenish-yellow couch with a light green throw pillow. I see two shallow light-colored baskets full of papers next to a vase of red poppies.

- *Listen and name the sounds you hear right now.* Now I hear the whooshing of my little heater and the soft thap, thap, thappity, thap of the computer keys. When the heater cuts off, I hear the computer's soft hum. Now I hear my dog stir, and the jingle of the tags on her collar. I hear a car passing in the street, and I can faintly hear children playing in the next block.

- *Be aware of smells.* Now I smell my spicy cup of tea and, yes, the dog could use a bath. I smell a slight musty odor coming from the carpet.

- *Pay attention to your physical sensations.* Now I feel my fingers moving on the keys and my wrists resting on the edge of the hard wooden desk. I feel the warmth of the steam from my tea. I feel my back and thighs resting against the chair, and I feel a bit of tension in my neck. I feel my breath—in, out, in, out. Now my neck is relaxing a little as I shift my feet. I feel my feet resting on the floor. (Getting in touch with the sensations in your feet can be really particularly helpful when you want to "ground" yourself. Try "breathing into your feet" as you gently and slowly inhale air into your lungs.)

- *Notice what you taste.* Right now I taste cloves and cinnamon in my tea.

If you want to go further in this exercise, deliberately increase the intensity of your five senses so that your attention is even more fully engaged. Describe what you see in greater detail, always remembering to stay in the here and now. Change your view by going into another room or taking a walk outside. Look in your refrigerator and describe everything you see. Watch a sunset from beginning to end, describing it as you go. Scrape an upholstered chair, a cardboard box, a plastic toy, or any other textured surface with your fingernails and carefully describe the different sounds you make. Turn on the faucet and listen to the myriad sounds within the splashing. Take a whiff of a strong odor, perhaps a sliced onion, perfume, or rubbing alcohol. Gently snap a rubber band on your wrist to give yourself a sharper physical sensation, or rub your face with a cold, wet washcloth. Taste something sweet, hot, or spicy. A courageous woman I know occasionally eats fireball candy to momentarily shut down some extraordinarily painful memories. But she doesn't stay away from herself for long. She returns to her inner work when she is ready to go on.

## 2. *Activate your prayerful imagination.*

Allow yourself to imagine the Holy One present with you. Don't limit yourself to seeing images with your mind's eye. Some people imagine by "hearing" things; others "have a sense" or "a feel" for what is going on. A few imagine by paying attention to how thoughts and ideas rearrange themselves into new patterns. Many combine different ways of imagining, so they might "see" images as well as "hear" sounds. Take some time with this initial imagining of Presence. Then ask the Holy One to seal up your feelings and memories for now but to preserve them for another day. Be quiet, further open your imagination if you can, and pay attention to what happens next. Is the Holy One willing to help you in this way? Many people have discovered the answer is yes.

Some who have prayed this "holding" prayer pictured Jesus carefully putting their feelings in a box or behind a locked door and standing guard over them. Others experienced their feelings and memories being covered with light. One person reported that her inner chaos was muffled by a "blanket of peace." Still others have had a sense that God's energy moved between them and their fears, making a sort of buffer zone.

Obviously I can't promise just how your prayer will be answered. I can tell you though, that many have been startled to discover that the Holy One actually seems to treasure the feelings and memories that seem so frightening. Furthermore, those who pray in this way often find themselves ready to continue with their work in the days or months ahead. Then they pray that God will unveil only the feelings they are ready for, or the ones that God wants to touch that day.

# *for* FURTHER READING

Morton T. Kelsey. *Dreams: A Way to Listen to God* was first published in 1977 and reissued by Paulist Press in 2002. In this groundbreaking book Father Kelsey suggests that ordinary people can work with their dreams. Written from a Jungian perspective.

Morton T. Kelsey. *God, Dreams, and Revelation: A Christian Interpretation of Dreams* was published by Augsburg Books in a revised and expanded edition in 1991. Presents a history of Christian dream interpretation.

Tilda Norberg. *Consenting to Grace: An Introduction to Gestalt Pastoral Care,* Penn House Press, 2006. See especially the sections on faith imagination and dreamwork.

Frederick "Fritz" Perls. *Gestalt Therapy Verbatim* was first published in 1969 by Real People Press and reissued by the Gestalt Journal Press in 1992. Contains many verbatim transcripts of dreamwork sessions with commentary by Dr. Perls.

# THANK YOU

To Noah Norberg-McClain, with love

Love to others in my family as well: Shana, Dan, Silas, Evelyn, Liz, James, Margaret, Alan, Paula, Kristin, Jane, Jorge John, Dora, Tex, Greg, Ron, Steve, Lori-Ann, and of course, my dear George. I am so grateful that all of you are in the world.

Special thanks, as always, to the bodacious women of Gestalt Pastoral Care Ecumenical Associates: Wanda Craner, Anne Cormier, Rhoda Glick, and Sara Goold. What would we do without one another? I'm also grateful to Yuri Ando, Linda Thomas, CJ Haury, and Betty Voigt for your wise input and thoughtful questions. I won't forget your unstinting help with teaching and getting things organized.

To the members of The Prayer House Community, your care and unfailing support has been a lifeline. As I write your names, I thank each of you: Kim Baldwin, Peter Chepaitis, Rhoda Glick, Debra Keller-Klimo, Gail Metzger, Rodney Miller, Ruth Ellen Ray, Lyn Reith, Donna Joy Schmid, Janet Stanley, Anna Tantsits, and Joyce Thomas. Thank you, Penny Gadzini, for helping me think through the Freud passages.

And to those who allowed your dream stories to be told, my deepest appreciation for your courage and generosity.

# ABOUT *the* AUTHOR

Tilda Norberg, a United Methodist clergywoman, is the founder of Gestalt Pastoral Care. This holistic form of pastoral counseling has roots in Gestalt psychotherapy, healing prayer, and spiritual companioning. In addition to her private practice, Tilda leads workshops and retreats for a variety of groups. For more information, visit www.gestaltpastoralcare.com.

Thomas Duncan Photography

Norberg is the author of the following books:

- *Gathered Together: Creating Personal Liturgies for Healing and Transformation*
- *Consenting to Grace: An Introduction to Gestalt Pastoral Care*
- *Ashes Transformed: Healing from Trauma*
- *Threadbear: A Story of Christian Healing for Adult Survivors of Sexual Abuse*

She coauthored, with Robert D. Webber, *Stretch Out Your Hand: Exploring Healing Prayer.*

Norberg is a graduate of Union Theological Seminary in New York City, The Gestalt Institute of Canada, and the Lomi School in San Francisco. She and her husband, the Reverend George McClain, live on Staten Island and are the parents of two grown children, Shana and Noah, and the proud grandparents of Silas.